Criminal Procedures

2012 Supplement

2012 Supplement

Criminal Procedures

Cases, Statutes, and Executive Materials

Fourth Edition

Marc L. Miller
Vice Dean and Ralph W. Bilby Professor of Law
University of Arizona

Ronald F. Wright
Needham P. Gulley Professor of Criminal Law
Wake Forest University

Wolters Kluwer
Law & Business

To contact Customer Service, e-mail customer.service@wolterskluwer.com, call 1-800-234-1660, fax 1-800-901-9075, or mail correspondence to:

Wolters Kluwer Law & Business
Attn: Order Department
PO Box 990
Frederick, MD 21705

Printed in the United States of America.

1 2 3 4 5 6 7 8 9 0

ISBN 978-0-7355-0992-4

About Wolters Kluwer Law & Business

Wolters Kluwer Law & Business is a leading global provider of intelligent information and digital solutions for legal and business professionals in key specialty areas, and respected educational resources for professors and law students. Wolters Kluwer Law & Business connects legal and business professionals as well as those in the education market with timely, specialized authoritative content and information-enabled solutions to support success through productivity, accuracy and mobility.

Serving customers worldwide, Wolters Kluwer Law & Business products include those under the Aspen Publishers, CCH, Kluwer Law International, Loislaw, Best Case, ftwilliam.com and MediRegs family of products.

CCH products have been a trusted resource since 1913, and are highly regarded resources for legal, securities, antitrust and trade regulation, government contracting, banking, pension, payroll, employment and labor, and healthcare reimbursement and compliance professionals.

Aspen Publishers products provide essential information to attorneys, business professionals and law students. Written by preeminent authorities, the product line offers analytical and practical information in a range of specialty practice areas from securities law and intellectual property to mergers and acquisitions and pension/benefits. Aspen's trusted legal education resources provide professors and students with high-quality, up-to-date and effective resources for successful instruction and study in all areas of the law.

Kluwer Law International products provide the global business community with reliable international legal information in English. Legal practitioners, corporate counsel and business executives around the world rely on Kluwer Law journals, looseleafs, books, and electronic products for comprehensive information in many areas of international legal practice.

Loislaw is a comprehensive online legal research product providing legal content to law firm practitioners of various specializations. Loislaw provides attorneys with the ability to quickly and efficiently find the necessary legal information they need, when and where they need it, by facilitating access to primary law as well as state-specific law, records, forms and treatises.

Best Case Solutions is the leading bankruptcy software product to the bankruptcy industry. It provides software and workflow tools to flawlessly streamline petition preparation and the electronic filing process, while timely incorporating ever-changing court requirements.

ftwilliam.com offers employee benefits professionals the highest quality plan documents (retirement, welfare and non-qualified) and government forms (5500/PBGC, 1099 and IRS) software at highly competitive prices.

MediRegs products provide integrated health care compliance content and software solutions for professionals in healthcare, higher education and life sciences, including professionals in accounting, law and consulting.

Wolters Kluwer Law & Business, a division of Wolters Kluwer, is headquartered in New York. Wolters Kluwer is a market-leading global information services company focused on professionals.

Contents

Preface

One function of a casebook supplement is to keep teachers and students current with recent events. In terms of basic doctrine, most aspects of criminal procedure have changed only modestly over the past few years. This is particularly true for a book, such as this one, that emphasizes nationwide trends within state criminal justice systems. Such nationwide changes take much longer to develop than any shifts in a single jurisdiction.

Nevertheless, these are remarkable times in criminal justice, and these remarkable events must become part of a vibrant criminal procedure course. In the long-term aftermath of the events of September 11, 2001, lawyers and judges in criminal courts all over the country continue to generate questions about how criminal procedure might change with the threat of terrorism in the background. The U.S. Supreme Court has proven remarkably active in the area for several years running, and the high state courts have added important insights of their own. These events are altering the law of *Miranda* warnings, the exclusionary rule, pretrial detention, and many other topics.

Some of the materials in this supplement will appear in the next edition; other materials may eventually disappear from the print format materials and move to the web site. Many decisions from the U.S. Supreme Court (along with some from the state supreme courts) seem on a first reading to make a dramatic shift in law and practice. However, after a year or two for reflection, some of those cases appear to be less important, because they merely restate or apply established concepts. A casebook supplement is a good opportunity to test the staying power of new cases, statutes, and policies.

This supplement is consistent with our larger goal of creating materials to extend the breadth and depth of the core casebook. We have also created internet-based pages for this casebook to enrich the resources available for students using this casebook. Our goal is not to create a single electronic coursebook. Instead, the electronic resources broaden, deepen, and enliven the core text.

The *Criminal Procedures* Web pages include materials allowing students to test and expand their knowledge, such as practice problems, exams, short excerpts of articles on criminal procedure, and "extension" topics to develop themes and sub-topics that receive passing attention in the printed text. The address for these pages is http://www.crimpro.com (or simply type "crimpro" in your browser). We welcome suggestions for materials to post on the Web pages or to publish in this printed supplement.

We hope you find that the casebook, this supplement, and the Web pages—together—offer a complete, coherent, and challenging set of tools for learning about criminal procedure.

Marc Miller
Ron Wright

July 2012

Table of Cases

Principal cases are in italic.
Principal Supreme Court cases are in bold.

Chapter 1

The Border of Criminal Procedure: Daily Interactions Between Citizens and Police

C. Control of Gangs and Kids

Page 11. Add the following material at the end of note 1.

See also State v. Gibson, 267 P.3d 645 (Alaska 2012) (defining emergency aid doctrine more narrowly under state constitution than the federal constitution allows; requires courts to consider police officers' subjective motives for making warrantless entry of home).

Page 27. Add the following material at the end of note 1.

Is there a meaningful difference between the powers of the police under the Chicago ordinance and the traditional police power to order pedestrians to disperse, accompanied by a possible arrest those who refuse for disorderly conduct? See Kimberly Winbush, Validity, Construction, and Application of State Statutes and Municipal Ordinances Proscribing Failure or Refusal to Obey Police Officer's

Order to Move On, or Disperse, on Street, as Disorderly Conduct, 52 A.L.R.6th 125 (2010).

Chapter 2

Brief Searches and Stops

A. Brief Investigative Stops of Suspects

1. Consensual Encounters and "Stops"

Page 56. Add the following material at the end of note 1.

See State v. Ashbaugh, 244 P.3d 360 (Ore. 2010) (suspect's subjective beliefs not relevant in establishing that a reasonable person would not feel free to leave).

Page 58. Add the following material at the end of note 1.

See also State v. Martin, 79 So. 3d 951 (La. 2011) (reviewing cases and refusing to adopt a per se rule converting consensual encounter into seizure whenever police retain suspect's documentation for warrants check).

3. Pretextual Stops

Page 79. Add the following material at the end of note 7.

See also Ashcroft v. al-Kidd, 131 S. Ct. 2074 (2011) (an arrest of a non-citizen under the federal material support statute was based on individualized suspicion that he was a material witness to a federal crime who would soon disappear unless he was detained; because the government made the showing required by law, the detainee could not invalidate the detention by showing that the true motive for his arrest was a Department of Justice policy to use the statute as a measure to strike preemptively against terrorism suspects).

Chapter 3

Full Searches of People and Places: Basic Concepts

C. Warrants

1. The Warrant Requirement and Exigent Circumstances

Page 180. Replace *Mann v. State* with the following material.

State and federal courts have wrestled with the extent to which police may take actions that generate exigent circumstances. In the following the case, the United States Supreme Court first addressed this issue. On first read, the U.S. Supreme Court opinion in *Kentucky v. King* may seem to eliminate the requirement of exigency as a matter of federal law. But the decision by the Supreme Court of Kentucky on remand reminds us that the U.S. Supreme Court opinion does not address the question of what information is sufficient to justify a warrantless search based on exigent circumstances.

Kentucky v. Hollis Deshaun King
131 S. Ct. 1849 (2011)

ALITO, J.[*]

It is well established that "exigent circumstances," including the need to prevent the destruction of evidence, permit police officers to conduct an otherwise permissible search without first obtaining a warrant. In this case, we consider whether this rule applies when police, by knocking on the door of a residence and announcing their presence, cause the occupants to attempt to destroy evidence. The Kentucky Supreme Court held that the exigent circumstances rule does not apply in the case at hand because the police should have foreseen that their conduct would prompt the occupants to attempt to destroy evidence. We reject this interpretation of the exigent circumstances rule. The conduct of the police prior to their entry into the apartment was entirely lawful. They did not violate the Fourth Amendment or threaten to do so. In such a situation, the exigent circumstances rule applies.

I ...

This case concerns the search of an apartment in Lexington, Kentucky. Police officers set up a controlled buy of crack cocaine outside an apartment complex. Undercover Officer Gibbons watched the deal take place from an unmarked car in a nearby parking lot. After the deal occurred, Gibbons radioed uniformed officers to move in on the suspect. He told the officers that the suspect was moving quickly toward the breezeway of an apartment building, and he urged them to "hurry up and get there" before the suspect entered an apartment.

In response to the radio alert, the uniformed officers drove into the nearby parking lot, left their vehicles, and ran to the breezeway. Just as they entered the breezeway, they heard a door shut and detected a very strong odor of burnt marijuana. At the end of the breezeway, the officers saw two apartments, one on the left and one on the right, and they did not know which apartment the suspect had entered. Gibbons had radioed that the suspect was running into the apartment on the right, but the officers did not hear this statement because they had already left their vehicles. Because they smelled marijuana smoke emanating from the apartment on the left, they approached the door of that apartment.

---

[*] Chief Justice Roberts and Justices Scalia, Kennedy, Thomas, Breyer, Sotomayor, and Kagan joined this opinion.

Officer Steven Cobb, one of the uniformed officers who approached the door, testified that the officers banged on the left apartment door "as loud as [they] could" and announced, "This is the police" or "Police, police, police." Cobb said that "as soon as [the officers] started banging on the door," they "could hear people inside moving," and "it sounded as [though] things were being moved inside the apartment." These noises, Cobb testified, led the officers to believe that drug-related evidence was about to be destroyed.

At that point, the officers announced that they "were going to make entry inside the apartment." Cobb then kicked in the door, the officers entered the apartment, and they found three people in the front room: respondent Hollis King, respondent's girlfriend, and a guest who was smoking marijuana. The officers performed a protective sweep of the apartment during which they saw marijuana and powder cocaine in plain view. In a subsequent search, they also discovered crack cocaine, cash, and drug paraphernalia.

Police eventually entered the apartment on the right. Inside, they found the suspected drug dealer who was the initial target of their investigation. ...

In the Fayette County Circuit Court, a grand jury charged respondent with trafficking in marijuana, first-degree trafficking in a controlled substance, and second-degree persistent felony offender status. Respondent filed a motion to suppress the evidence from the warrantless search, but the Circuit Court denied the motion. ... The Supreme Court of Kentucky reversed. ... To determine whether police impermissibly created the exigency, the Supreme Court of Kentucky announced a two-part test. First, the court held, police cannot "deliberately create the exigent circumstances with the bad faith intent to avoid the warrant requirement." Second, even absent bad faith, the court concluded, police may not rely on exigent circumstances if "it was reasonably foreseeable that the investigative tactics employed by the police would create the exigent circumstances." Although the court found no evidence of bad faith, it held that exigent circumstances could not justify the search because it was reasonably foreseeable that the occupants would destroy evidence when the police knocked on the door and announced their presence. ...

II

Although the text of the Fourth Amendment does not specify when a

7

search warrant must be obtained, this Court has inferred that a warrant must generally be secured. It is a basic principle of Fourth Amendment law ... that searches and seizures inside a home without a warrant are presumptively unreasonable. But we have also recognized that this presumption may be overcome in some circumstances because the ultimate touchstone of the Fourth Amendment is "reasonableness." Accordingly, the warrant requirement is subject to certain reasonable exceptions.

One well-recognized exception applies when "the exigencies of the situation" make the needs of law enforcement so compelling that a warrantless search is objectively reasonable under the Fourth Amendment. This Court has identified several exigencies that may justify a warrantless search of a home. Under the "emergency aid" exception, for example, officers may enter a home without a warrant to render emergency assistance to an injured occupant or to protect an occupant from imminent injury. Police officers may enter premises without a warrant when they are in hot pursuit of a fleeing suspect. And—what is relevant here—the need to prevent the imminent destruction of evidence has long been recognized as a sufficient justification for a warrantless search. ...

Over the years, lower courts have developed an exception to the exigent circumstances rule, the so-called "police-created exigency" doctrine. Under this doctrine, police may not rely on the need to prevent destruction of evidence when that exigency was "created" or "manufactured" by the conduct of the police. In applying this exception for the creation or manufacturing of an exigency by the police, courts require something more than mere proof that fear of detection by the police caused the destruction of evidence. An additional showing is obviously needed because, ... in some sense the police always create the exigent circumstances. That is to say, in the vast majority of cases in which evidence is destroyed by persons who are engaged in illegal conduct, the reason for the destruction is fear that the evidence will fall into the hands of law enforcement. ... Consequently, a rule that precludes the police from making a warrantless entry to prevent the destruction of evidence whenever their conduct causes the exigency would unreasonably shrink the reach of this well-established exception to the warrant requirement. Presumably for the purpose of avoiding such a result, the lower courts have held that the police-created exigency doctrine requires more than simple causation, but the lower courts have not agreed on the test to be applied....

III
A

[The] answer to the question presented in this case follows directly and clearly from the principle that permits warrantless searches in the first place. As previously noted, warrantless searches are allowed when the circumstances make it reasonable, within the meaning of the Fourth Amendment, to dispense with the warrant requirement. Therefore, the answer to the question before us is that the exigent circumstances rule justifies a warrantless search when the conduct of the police preceding the exigency is reasonable in the same sense. Where, as here, the police did not create the exigency by engaging or threatening to engage in conduct that violates the Fourth Amendment, warrantless entry to prevent the destruction of evidence is reasonable and thus allowed.[4]

We have taken a similar approach in other cases involving warrantless searches. For example, we have held that law enforcement officers may seize evidence in plain view, provided that they have not violated the Fourth Amendment in arriving at the spot from which the observation of the evidence is made.... So long as this prerequisite is satisfied, however, it does not matter that the officer who makes the observation may have gone to the spot from which the evidence was seen with the hope of being able to view and seize the evidence. Instead, the Fourth Amendment requires only that the steps preceding the seizure be lawful.

Similarly, officers may seek consent-based encounters if they are lawfully present in the place where the consensual encounter occurs. See INS v. Delgado, 466 U.S. 210, 217, n. 5 (1984) (noting that officers who entered into consent-based encounters with employees in a factory building were "lawfully present [in the factory] pursuant to consent or a warrant"). If consent is freely given, it makes no difference that an officer may have approached the person with the hope or expectation of obtaining consent....

---

[4] There is a strong argument to be made that, at least in most circumstances, the exigent circumstances rule should not apply where the police, without a warrant or any legally sound basis for a warrantless entry, threaten that they will enter without permission unless admitted. In this case, however, no such actual threat was made, and therefore we have no need to reach that question.

B

Some lower courts have adopted a rule that is similar to the one that we recognize today. But others, including the Kentucky Supreme Court, have imposed additional requirements that are unsound and that we now reject.

Bad faith. Some courts, including the Kentucky Supreme Court, ask whether law enforcement officers deliberately created the exigent circumstances with the bad faith intent to avoid the warrant requirement. This approach is fundamentally inconsistent with our Fourth Amendment jurisprudence. Our cases have repeatedly rejected a subjective approach, asking only whether the circumstances, viewed *objectively,* justify the action. Indeed, we have never held, outside limited contexts such as an inventory search or administrative inspection, that an officer's motive invalidates objectively justifiable behavior under the Fourth Amendment. Whren v. United States, 517 U.S. 806, 812 (1996). ...

Reasonable foreseeability. Some courts, again including the Kentucky Supreme Court, hold that police may not rely on an exigency if it was reasonably foreseeable that the investigative tactics employed by the police would create the exigent circumstances. Mann v. State, 357 Ark. 159, 172, 161 S.W.3d 826, 834 (2004)). Courts applying this test have invalidated warrantless home searches on the ground that it was reasonably foreseeable that police officers, by knocking on the door and announcing their presence, would lead a drug suspect to destroy evidence.

Contrary to this reasoning, however, we have rejected the notion that police may seize evidence without a warrant only when they come across the evidence by happenstance.... Adoption of a reasonable foreseeability test would also introduce an unacceptable degree of unpredictability. For example, whenever law enforcement officers knock on the door of premises occupied by a person who may be involved in the drug trade, there is *some* possibility that the occupants may possess drugs and may seek to destroy them. Under a reasonable foreseeability test, it would be necessary to quantify the degree of predictability that must be reached before the police-created exigency doctrine comes into play.

A simple example illustrates the difficulties that such an approach would produce. Suppose that the officers in the present case did not smell marijuana smoke and thus knew only that there was a 50% chance that the fleeing suspect had entered the apartment on the left rather than the apartment on the right. Under those circumstances, would it have been reasonably foreseeable that the occupants of the apartment on the left would seek to destroy evidence upon learning that the police were at the door? Or suppose that the officers knew only that the suspect had disappeared into one of the apartments on a floor with 3, 5, 10, or even 20 units? If the police chose a door at random and knocked for the purpose of asking the occupants if they knew a person who fit the description of the suspect, would it have been reasonably foreseeable that the occupants would seek to destroy evidence?

We have noted that the calculus of reasonableness must embody allowance for the fact that police officers are often forced to make split-second judgments—in circumstances that are tense, uncertain, and rapidly evolving. The reasonable foreseeability test would create unacceptable and unwarranted difficulties for law enforcement officers who must make quick decisions in the field, as well as for judges who would be required to determine after the fact whether the destruction of evidence in response to a knock on the door was reasonably foreseeable based on what the officers knew at the time.

Probable cause and time to secure a warrant. Some courts, in applying the police-created exigency doctrine, fault law enforcement officers if, after acquiring evidence that is sufficient to establish probable cause to search particular premises, the officers do not seek a warrant but instead knock on the door and seek either to speak with an occupant or to obtain consent to search. This approach unjustifiably interferes with legitimate law enforcement strategies. There are many entirely proper reasons why police may not want to seek a search warrant as soon as the bare minimum of evidence needed to establish probable cause is acquired. Without attempting to provide a comprehensive list of these reasons, we note a few.

First, the police may wish to speak with the occupants of a dwelling before deciding whether it is worthwhile to seek authorization for a search. They may think that a short and simple conversation may obviate the need to apply for and execute a warrant. Second, the police may want to ask an occupant of the premises for consent to search because doing so is simpler, faster, and less burdensome than applying for a warrant. A consensual search also may result in considerably less inconvenience and embarrassment to the occupants than a search conducted pursuant to a warrant. Third, law enforcement officers may wish to obtain more evidence before submitting what might otherwise be considered a marginal warrant application. Fourth, prosecutors may wish to wait until they acquire evidence that can justify a search that is broader in scope than the search that a judicial officer is likely to authorize based on the evidence then available. And finally, in many cases, law enforcement may not want to execute a search that will disclose the existence of an investigation because doing so may interfere with the acquisition of additional evidence against those already under suspicion or evidence about additional but as yet unknown participants in a criminal scheme.

[Law] enforcement officers are under no constitutional duty to call a halt to criminal investigation the moment they have the minimum evidence to establish probable cause. Faulting the police for failing to apply for a search warrant at the earliest possible time after obtaining probable cause imposes a duty that is nowhere to be found in the Constitution.

Standard or good investigative tactics. Finally, some lower court cases suggest that law enforcement officers may be found to have created or manufactured an exigency if the court concludes that the course of their investigation was contrary to standard or good law enforcement practices (or to the policies or practices of their jurisdictions). This approach fails to provide clear guidance for law enforcement officers and authorizes courts to make judgments on matters that are the province of those who are responsible for federal and state law enforcement agencies.

C

Respondent argues for a rule that differs from those discussed above, but his rule is also flawed. Respondent contends that law enforcement officers impermissibly create an exigency when they "engage in conduct that would cause a reasonable person to believe that entry is imminent and inevitable." In respondent's view, relevant factors include the officers' tone of voice in announcing their presence and the forcefulness of their knocks. But the ability of law enforcement officers to respond to an exigency cannot turn on such subtleties.

Police officers may have a very good reason to announce their presence loudly and to knock on the door with some force. A forceful knock may be necessary to alert the occupants that someone is at the door. Furthermore, unless police officers identify themselves loudly enough, occupants may not know who is at their doorstep.... Citizens who are startled by an unexpected knock on the door or by the sight of unknown persons in plain clothes on their doorstep may be relieved to learn that these persons are police officers. Others may appreciate the opportunity to make an informed decision about whether to answer the door to the police.

If respondent's test were adopted, it would be extremely difficult for police officers to know how loudly they may announce their presence or how forcefully they may knock on a door without running afoul of the police-created exigency rule. And in most cases, it would be nearly impossible for a court to determine whether that threshold had been passed. The Fourth Amendment does not require the nebulous and impractical test that respondent proposes.

D

For these reasons, we conclude that the exigent circumstances rule applies when the police do not gain entry to premises by means of an actual or threatened violation of the Fourth Amendment. This holding provides ample protection for the privacy rights that the Amendment protects.

When law enforcement officers who are not armed with a warrant knock on a door, they do no more than any private citizen might do. And whether the person who knocks on the door and requests the opportunity to speak is a police officer or a private citizen, the occupant has no obligation to open the door or to speak. When the police knock on a door but the occupants choose not to respond or to speak, the investigation will have reached a conspicuously low point, and the occupants will have the kind of warning that even the most elaborate security system cannot provide. And even if an occupant chooses to open the door and speak with the officers, the occupant need not allow the officers to enter the premises and may refuse to answer any questions at any time.

Occupants who choose not to stand on their constitutional rights but instead elect to attempt to destroy evidence have only themselves to blame for the warrantless exigent-circumstances search that may ensue.

IV

We now apply our interpretation of the police-created exigency doctrine to the facts of this case.... We need not decide whether exigent circumstances existed in this case. Any warrantless entry based on exigent circumstances must, of course, be supported by a genuine exigency. The trial court and the Kentucky Court of Appeals found that there was a real exigency in this case, but the Kentucky Supreme Court expressed doubt on this issue, observing that there was "certainly some question as to whether the sound of persons moving [inside the apartment] was sufficient to establish that evidence was being destroyed." The Kentucky Supreme Court assumed for the purpose of argument that exigent circumstances existed, and it held that the police had impermissibly manufactured the exigency. We, too, assume for purposes of argument that an exigency existed....

In this case, we see no evidence that the officers either violated the Fourth Amendment or threatened to do so prior to the point when they entered the apartment. Officer Cobb testified without contradiction that the officers "banged on the door as loud as [they] could" and announced either "Police, police, police" or "This is the police." This conduct was entirely consistent with the Fourth Amendment, and we are aware of no other evidence that might show that the officers either violated the Fourth Amendment or threatened to do so (for example, by announcing that they would break down the door if the occupants did not open the door voluntarily). Respondent argues that the officers "demanded" entry to the apartment, but he has not pointed to any evidence in the record that supports this assertion....

Finally, respondent claims that the officers "explained to [the occupants that the officers] were going to make entry inside the apartment," but the record is clear that the officers did not make this statement until after the exigency arose. As Officer Cobb testified, the officers "knew that there was possibly something that was going to be destroyed inside the apartment," and "at that point, they explained that they were going to make entry." Given that this announcement was made *after* the exigency arose, it could not have created the exigency.

Like the court below, we assume for purposes of argument that an exigency existed. Because the officers in this case did not violate or threaten to violate the Fourth Amendment prior to the exigency, we hold that the exigency justified the warrantless search of the apartment....

GINSBURG, J., dissenting.

The Court today arms the police with a way routinely to dishonor the Fourth Amendment's warrant requirement in drug cases. In lieu of presenting their evidence to a neutral magistrate, police officers may now knock, listen, then break the door down, nevermind that they had ample time to obtain a warrant. I dissent from the Court's reduction of the Fourth Amendment's force....

The question presented: May police, who could pause to gain the approval of a neutral magistrate, dispense with the need to get a warrant by themselves creating exigent circumstances? I would answer no, as did the Kentucky Supreme Court. The urgency must exist, I would rule, when the police come on the scene, not subsequent to their arrival, prompted by their own conduct....

In no quarter does the Fourth Amendment apply with greater force than in our homes, our most private space which, for centuries, has been regarded as entitled to special protection.... How "secure" do our homes remain if police, armed with no warrant, can pound on doors at will and, on hearing sounds indicative of things moving, forcibly enter and search for evidence of unlawful activity? ...

The existence of a genuine emergency depends not only on the state of necessity at the time of the warrantless search; it depends, first and foremost, on actions taken by the police preceding the warrantless search. Wasting a clear opportunity to obtain a warrant, therefore, disentitles the officer from relying on subsequent exigent circumstances.

Under an appropriately reined-in "emergency" or "exigent circumstances" exception, the result in this case should not be in doubt. The target of the investigation's entry into the building, and the smell of marijuana seeping under the apartment door into the hallway, the Kentucky Supreme Court rightly determined, gave the police probable cause sufficient to obtain a warrant to search the apartment. As that court observed, nothing made it impracticable for the police to post officers on the premises while proceeding to obtain a warrant authorizing their entry....

Hollis Deshaun King v. Commonwealth
___ S.W. 3d ___, 2012 WL 1450081 (Ky. 2012)

SCHRODER, J.

This case is before this Court on remand from the United States Supreme Court, Kentucky v. King, 563 U.S. ___ (2011), rev'g King v. Commonwealth, 302 S.W.3d 649 (Ky. 2010), to determine whether exigent circumstances existed when police made a warrantless entry into an apartment occupied by Appellant Hollis King. We conclude that the Commonwealth has failed to show circumstances establishing the imminent destruction of evidence. We therefore reverse the original ruling of the circuit court and remand....

Assuming as this Court did that exigent circumstances existed, the U.S. Supreme Court held that police may rely on exigent circumstances so long as "the police did not create the exigency by engaging or threatening to engage in conduct that violates the Fourth Amendment...." Because the police in this case did not engage in any such conduct, the Supreme Court reversed this Court, but held that any question "about whether an exigency actually existed is better addressed by the Kentucky Supreme Court on remand." It is this issue which we now address.

We begin by noting that the touchstone of the Fourth Amendment is reasonableness, which is measured in objective terms by examining the totality of the circumstances. Under the Fourth Amendment to the United States Constitution, in the absence of consent, police may not conduct a warrantless search or seizure within a private residence without both probable cause and exigent circumstances. [In this case, it is undisputed that the smell of marijuana created the requisite probable cause.] Any other search is per se unreasonable. The Commonwealth carries the burden to demonstrate that the warrantless entry falls within a recognized exception to the warrant requirement....

Because police were not in hot pursuit of a fleeing suspect, i.e., the crack cocaine dealer, our analysis naturally focuses on imminent destruction of evidence and the totality of the circumstances from the time police smelled marijuana emanating from the back left apartment.

Turning to the question at hand, we conclude that the Commonwealth failed to meet its burden of demonstrating exigent circumstances justifying a warrantless entry. During the suppression hearing, Officer Cobb repeatedly referred to the "possible" destruction of evidence. He stated that he heard people moving inside the apartment, and that this was "the same kind of movements we've heard inside" when other suspects have destroyed evidence. Cobb never articulated the specific sounds he heard which led him to believe that evidence was about to be destroyed.

In fact, the sounds as described at the suppression hearing were indistinguishable from ordinary household sounds, and were consistent with the natural and reasonable result of a knock on the door. Nothing in the record suggests that the sounds officers heard were anything more than the occupants preparing to answer the door.

The police officers' subjective belief that evidence was being (or about to be) destroyed is not supported by the record, and this Court cannot conclude that the belief was objectively reasonable. No exigency

16

is created simply because there is probable cause to believe that a serious crime has been committed. Exigent circumstances do not deal with mere possibilities, and the Commonwealth must show something more than a possibility that evidence is being destroyed to defeat the presumption of an unreasonable search and seizure.

[This] Court concludes that exigent circumstances did not exist when police made a warrantless entry of the apartment occupied by Appellant King. Therefore, the denial of King's motion to suppress evidence is reversed, and King's judgment of conviction stands vacated.

Page 184. Add the following material after note 1.

2. *Caveat emptor*. It is easy to misread the U.S. Supreme Court opinion in *King* and to conclude that as a matter of federal law exigent circumstances can now be created by police and will be found at will. As the decision by the Kentucky Supreme Court on remand suggests, state and federal courts since *King* have not read the opinion this way, and have regularly concluded that exigent circumstances do not exist, even when there is abundant evidence to find that probable cause exists. See, e.g., State v. Aguilar, 267 P.3d 1193 (Ariz. Ct. App. 2011) (noting that "warrantless entry was lawful only if both probable cause and exigent circumstances existed," and while there was probable cause, the fact that none of the occupants opened the door when the police officers initially demanded that the door be opened, while one occupant peeked outside the motel window, "did not give rise to an exigency justifying a warrantless entry.")

In addition, states that have "police created exigency" tests may retain them as a matter of state constitutional law. Courts may also broadly interpret the new standard in *King* that prohibits police from "engaging or threatening to engage in conduct that violates the Fourth Amendment." Therefore as a jurisprudential matter *King* already serves as a reminder that for any one decision is it necessary to consider the narrowest and broadest holding; the path a doctrine takes can only be determined by future decisions. See Edward Levi, An Introduction to Legal Reasoning (1962).

Moreover, the doctrinal impact must be distinguished from the impact on the streets, where police departments and district attorneys offices may tread warily around new or complex avenues for police to conduct seizures and searches, especially where functional "safe harbors" exist. See, e.g., Corey Fleming Hirokawa, Making the "Law of the Land" The Law On the Street: How Police Academies Teach Evolving Fourth Amendment Law, 49 Emory L.J. 295 (2000); Emily Ayn Ward, From Pen to Patrol: How Arizona Law Enforcement Applied Carrillo v. Houser, 53 Ariz. L. Rev. 345 (2011).

Chapter 4

Searches in Recurring Contexts

A. *"Persons"*

2. Intrusive Body Searches

Page 250. Add this material at the end of note 1.

See Florence v. Board of Chosen Freeholders, 132 S. Ct. 1510 (2012) (arrestee for failure to appear at hearing to enforce a fine was subjected, like every other detainee entering the jail, to strip search that included inspection of genitals and body openings; search policy did not violate Fourth Amendment).

B. *"Houses" and Other Places*

3. Schools and Prisons

Page 291. Add this material at the end of note 1.

See Florence v. Board of Chosen Freeholders, 132 S. Ct. 1510 (2012) (all arrestees were subjected, upon entry to jail facility, to strip search that included inspection of genitals and body openings; search policy did not violate Fourth Amendment).

Chapter 6

Remedies for Unreasonable Searches and Seizures

A. *Origins of the Exclusionary Rule*

Page 399. Add this material at the end of note 4.

See Kenworthey Bilz, Dirty Hands or Deterrence? An Experimental Examination of the Exclusionary Rule, 9 J. Empirical Legal Studies 149 (2012) (participants in experiment are sensitive to police officer's motive but not to alternative means of punishing those officers, suggesting support for integrity justification for exclusionary rule); Melanie D. Wilson, Improbable Cause: A Case for Judging Police by a More Majestic Standard, 15 Berk. J. Crim. L. 259 (2010) (empirical study of one federal district court over two years; author concludes that judges are probably perpetuating police perjury and calls for use of exclusionary rule for purposes of judicial and police integrity).

Page 400. Add this material at the end of note 6.

See State v. Torres, 262 P.3d 1006 (Haw. 2011) (where state seeks to admit evidence obtained in another jurisdiction, court must give "due consideration" to state constitution; court declines to declare categorically that evidence obtained elsewhere in violation of Hawaii state constitution must always be excluded).

B. Limitations on the Exclusionary Rule

1. Evidence Obtained in "Good Faith"

Page 408. Add this material at the end of note 2.

See also Messerschmidt v. Millender, 132 S. Ct. 1235 (2012) (fact that detective asked for review of warrant application by police supervisors and prosecutor before submitting it to magistrate is relevant in determining objective good faith reliance on warrant).

Page 411. Add this material before the notes.

Willie Gene Davis v. United States
131 S. Ct. 2419 (2011)

ALITO, J.[*]

The Fourth Amendment protects the right to be free from "unreasonable searches and seizures," but it is silent about how this right is to be enforced. To supplement the bare text, this Court created the exclusionary rule, a deterrent sanction that bars the prosecution from introducing evidence obtained by way of a Fourth Amendment violation. The question here is whether to apply this sanction when the police conduct a search in compliance with binding precedent that is later overruled. Because suppression would do nothing to deter police misconduct in these circumstances, and because it would come at a high cost to both the truth and the public safety, we hold that searches conducted in objectively reasonable reliance on binding appellate precedent are not subject to the exclusionary rule.

I

The question presented arises in this case as a result of a shift in our Fourth Amendment jurisprudence on searches of automobiles incident to arrests of recent occupants. [The opinion then described the facts and holding in New York v. Belton, 453 U.S. 454 (1981)].

---

[*] Chief Justice Roberts and Justices Scalia, Kennedy, Thomas, and Kagan joined this opinion.

For years, *Belton* was widely understood to have set down a simple, bright-line rule. Numerous courts read the decision to authorize automobile searches incident to arrests of recent occupants, regardless of whether the arrestee in any particular case was within reaching distance of the vehicle at the time of the search. Even after the arrestee had stepped out of the vehicle and had been subdued by police, the prevailing understanding was that *Belton* still authorized a substantially contemporaneous search of the automobile's passenger compartment.

Not every court, however, agreed with this reading of *Belton*. In State v. Gant, 162 P.3d 640 (Ariz. 2007), the Arizona Supreme Court considered an automobile search conducted after the vehicle's occupant had been arrested, handcuffed, and locked in a patrol car. The court distinguished *Belton* as a case in which "four unsecured" arrestees "presented an immediate risk of loss of evidence and an obvious threat to a lone officer's safety." The court held that where no such exigencies exist—where the arrestee has been subdued and the scene secured—the rule of *Belton* does not apply.

[The opinion then described the reasoning of the majority, dissenting, and concurring opinions in Arizona v. Gant, 556 U.S. 332 (2009). The] Court adopted a new, two-part rule under which an automobile search incident to a recent occupant's arrest is constitutional (1) if the arrestee is within reaching distance of the vehicle during the search, or (2) if the police have reason to believe that the vehicle contains "evidence relevant to the crime of arrest." ...

The search at issue in this case took place a full two years before this Court announced its new rule in *Gant*. On an April evening in 2007, police officers in Greenville, Alabama, conducted a routine traffic stop that eventually resulted in the arrests of driver Stella Owens (for driving while intoxicated) and passenger Willie Davis (for giving a false name to police). The police handcuffed both Owens and Davis, and they placed the arrestees in the back of separate patrol cars. The police then searched the passenger compartment of Owens's vehicle and found a revolver inside Davis's jacket pocket.

Davis was indicted in the Middle District of Alabama on one count of possession of a firearm by a convicted felon. In his motion to suppress the revolver, Davis acknowledged that the officers' search fully complied with existing Eleventh Circuit precedent. Like most courts, the Eleventh Circuit had long read *Belton* to establish a bright-line rule authorizing substantially contemporaneous vehicle searches incident to arrests of recent occupants. Davis recognized that the District Court was obligated to follow this precedent, but he raised a Fourth Amendment challenge to preserve "the issue for review" on appeal.

While Davis's appeal was pending, this Court decided *Gant*. The Eleventh Circuit, in the opinion below, applied *Gant*'s new rule and held that the vehicle search incident to Davis's arrest violated his Fourth Amendment rights. As for whether this constitutional violation warranted suppression, the Eleventh Circuit viewed that as a separate issue that turned on the potential of exclusion to deter wrongful police conduct. The court concluded that penalizing the arresting officer for following binding appellate precedent would do nothing to deter Fourth Amendment violations. It therefore declined to apply the exclusionary rule and affirmed Davis's conviction. We granted certiorari.

II

[The exclusionary] rule's sole purpose, we have repeatedly held, is to deter future Fourth Amendment violations. Our cases have thus limited the rule's operation to situations in which this purpose is thought most efficaciously served. Where suppression fails to yield "appreciable deterrence," exclusion is clearly unwarranted.

Real deterrent value is a necessary condition for exclusion, but it is not a sufficient one. The analysis must also account for the substantial social costs generated by the rule. Exclusion exacts a heavy toll on both the judicial system and society at large. It almost always requires courts to ignore reliable, trustworthy evidence bearing on guilt or innocence. And its bottom-line effect, in many cases, is to suppress the truth and set the criminal loose in the community without punishment. Our cases hold that society must swallow this bitter pill when necessary, but only as a "last resort." Hudson v. Michigan, 547 U.S. 586, 591 (2006). For exclusion to be appropriate, the deterrence benefits of suppression must outweigh its heavy costs.

Admittedly, there was a time when our exclusionary-rule cases were not nearly so discriminating in their approach to the doctrine. Expansive dicta in several decisions suggested that the rule was a self-executing mandate implicit in the Fourth Amendment itself. See Olmstead v. United States, 277 U.S. 438, 462 (1928) (remarking on the "striking outcome of the *Weeks* case" that "the Fourth Amendment, although not referring to or limiting the use of evidence in courts, really forbade its introduction"); Mapp v. Ohio, 367 U.S. 643, 655 (1961) (All evidence obtained by searches and seizures "in violation of the Constitution is, by that same authority, inadmissible in a state court"). … In time, however, we came to acknowledge the exclusionary rule for what it undoubtedly is—a judicially created remedy of this Court's own making. We abandoned the old, reflexive application of the doctrine, and imposed a more rigorous weighing of its costs and deterrence benefits. See United States v. Calandra, 414 U.S. 338 (1974). In a line of cases beginning with United States v. Leon, 468 U.S. 897 (1984), we also recalibrated our cost-benefit analysis in exclusion cases to focus the inquiry on the "flagrancy of the police misconduct" at issue.

The basic insight of the *Leon* line of cases is that the deterrence benefits of exclusion vary with the culpability of the law enforcement conduct at issue. When the police exhibit "deliberate," "reckless," or "grossly negligent" disregard for Fourth Amendment rights, the deterrent value of exclusion is strong and tends to outweigh the resulting costs. Herring v. United States, 555 U.S. 135, 144 (2009). But when the police act with an objectively "reasonable good-faith belief" that their conduct is lawful, *Leon, supra,* at 909, or when their conduct involves only simple, "isolated" negligence, *Herring, supra,* at 137, the deterrence rationale loses much of its force, and exclusion cannot "pay its way."

The Court has over time applied this "good-faith" exception across a range of cases. *Leon* itself, for example, held that the exclusionary rule does not apply when the police conduct a search in "objectively reasonable reliance" on a warrant later held invalid. The error in such a case rests with the issuing magistrate, not the police officer, and punishing the errors of judges is not the office of the exclusionary rule. *See* also Massachusetts v. Sheppard, 468 U.S. 981 (1984) (companion case declining to apply exclusionary rule where warrant held invalid as a result of judge's clerical error).

Other good-faith cases have sounded a similar theme. Illinois v. Krull, 480 U.S. 340 (1987), extended the good-faith exception to searches conducted in reasonable reliance on subsequently invalidated statutes. In Arizona v. Evans, 514 U.S. 1 (1995), the Court applied the good-faith exception in a case where the police reasonably relied on erroneous information concerning an arrest warrant in a database maintained by judicial employees. Most recently, in Herring v. United States, 555 U.S. 135 (2009), we extended *Evans* in a case where *police* employees erred in maintaining records in a warrant database. Isolated, nonrecurring police negligence, we determined, lacks the culpability required to justify the harsh sanction of exclusion.

III

The question in this case is whether to apply the exclusionary rule when the police conduct a search in objectively reasonable reliance on binding judicial precedent. At the time of the search at issue here, we had not yet decided Arizona v. Gant, 556 U.S. 332 (2009), and the Eleventh Circuit had interpreted our decision in New York v. Belton, 453 U.S. 454 (1984), to establish a bright-line rule authorizing the search of a vehicle's passenger compartment incident to a recent occupant's arrest. United States v. Gonzalez, 71 F.3d 819, 825 (11th Cir. 1996). The search incident to Davis's arrest in this case followed the Eleventh Circuit's *Gonzalez* precedent to the letter. Although the search turned out to be unconstitutional under *Gant,* all agree that the officers' conduct was in strict compliance with then-binding Circuit law and was not culpable in any way.

Under our exclusionary-rule precedents, this acknowledged absence of police culpability dooms Davis's claim. Police practices trigger the harsh sanction of exclusion only when they are deliberate enough to yield meaningful deterrence, and culpable enough to be worth the price paid by the justice system. The conduct of the officers here was neither of these things. The officers who conducted the search did not violate Davis's Fourth Amendment rights deliberately, recklessly, or with gross negligence. Nor does this case involve any recurring or systemic negligence on the part of law enforcement. The police acted in strict compliance with binding precedent, and their behavior was not wrongful. Unless the exclusionary rule is to become a strict-liability regime, it can have no application in this case....

About all that exclusion would deter in this case is conscientious police work. Responsible law-enforcement officers will take care to learn what is required of them under Fourth Amendment precedent and will conform their conduct to these rules. But by the same token, when binding appellate precedent specifically *authorizes* a particular police practice, well-trained officers will and should use that tool to fulfill their crime-detection and public-safety responsibilities.... The deterrent effect of exclusion in such a case can only be to discourage the officer from doing his duty.

That is not the kind of deterrence the exclusionary rule seeks to foster. We have stated before, and we reaffirm today, that the harsh sanction of exclusion should not be applied to deter objectively reasonable law enforcement activity. Evidence obtained during a search conducted in reasonable reliance on binding precedent is not subject to the exclusionary rule.

IV

Justice Breyer's dissent and Davis argue that, although the police conduct in this case was in no way culpable, other considerations should prevent the good-faith exception from applying. We are not persuaded.

A ...

The principal argument of both the dissent and Davis is that the exclusionary rule's availability to enforce new Fourth Amendment precedent is a retroactivity issue, see Griffith v. Kentucky, 479 U.S. 314 (1987), not a good-faith issue. They contend that applying the good-faith exception where police have relied on overruled precedent effectively revives the discarded retroactivity regime of Linkletter v. Walker, 381 U.S. 618 (1965).

In *Linkletter,* we held that the retroactive effect of a new constitutional rule of criminal procedure should be determined on a case-by-case weighing of interests. For each new rule, *Linkletter* required courts to consider a three-factor balancing test that looked to the "purpose" of the new rule, "reliance" on the old rule by law enforcement and others, and the effect retroactivity would have "on the administration of justice." After weighing the merits and demerits in each case, courts decided whether and to what extent a new rule should be given retroactive effect....

Over time, *Linkletter* proved difficult to apply in a consistent, coherent way. Individual applications of the standard produced strikingly divergent results.... Justice Harlan in particular, who had endorsed the *Linkletter* standard early on, offered a strong critique in which he argued that "basic judicial" norms required full retroactive application of new rules to all cases still subject to direct review. Eventually, and after more than 20 years of toil under *Linkletter,* the Court adopted Justice Harlan's view and held that newly announced rules of constitutional criminal procedure must apply "retroactively to all cases, state or federal, pending on direct review or not yet final, with no exception." *Griffith, supra,* at 328. ...

The dissent and Davis argue that applying the good-faith exception in this case is incompatible with our retroactivity precedent under *Griffith*. We think this argument conflates what are two distinct doctrines.

Our retroactivity jurisprudence is concerned with whether, as a categorical matter, a new rule is available on direct review as a *potential* ground for relief. Retroactive application under *Griffith* lifts what would otherwise be a categorical bar to obtaining redress for the government's violation of a newly announced constitutional rule. Retroactive application does not, however, determine what "appropriate remedy" (if any) the defendant should obtain. See Powell v. Nevada, 511 U.S. 79, 84 (1994) (noting that it "does not necessarily follow" from retroactive application of a new rule that the defendant will gain relief). Remedy is a separate, analytically distinct issue. As a result, the retroactive application of a new rule of substantive Fourth Amendment law *raises* the question whether a suppression remedy applies; it does not answer that question.

When this Court announced its decision in *Gant,* Davis's conviction had not yet become final on direct review. *Gant* therefore applies retroactively to this case. Davis may invoke its newly announced rule of substantive Fourth Amendment law as a basis for seeking relief. The question, then, becomes one of remedy, and on that issue Davis seeks application of the exclusionary rule. But exclusion of evidence does not automatically follow from the fact that a Fourth Amendment violation occurred. The remedy is subject to exceptions and applies only where its purpose is effectively advanced.

[Suppression would] be inappropriate, the dissent and Davis acknowledge, if the inevitable-discovery exception were applicable in this case. The good-faith exception, however, is no less an established limit on the *remedy* of exclusion than is inevitable discovery. Its application here neither contravenes *Griffith* nor denies retroactive effect to *Gant*. ...

B

Davis also contends that applying the good-faith exception to searches conducted in reliance on binding precedent will stunt the development of Fourth Amendment law. With no possibility of suppression, criminal defendants will have no incentive, Davis maintains, to request that courts overrule precedent. ...

This argument is difficult to reconcile with our modern

understanding of the role of the exclusionary rule. We have never held that facilitating the overruling of precedent is a relevant consideration in an exclusionary-rule case. Rather, we have said time and again that the *sole* purpose of the exclusionary rule is to deter misconduct by law enforcement....

And in any event, applying the good-faith exception in this context will not prevent judicial reconsideration of prior Fourth Amendment precedents. In most instances, as in this case, the precedent sought to be challenged will be a decision of a Federal Court of Appeals or State Supreme Court. But a good-faith exception for objectively reasonable reliance on binding precedent will not prevent review and correction of such decisions. This Court reviews criminal convictions from 12 Federal Courts of Appeals, 50 state courts of last resort, and the District of Columbia Court of Appeals. If one or even many of these courts uphold a particular type of search or seizure, defendants in jurisdictions in which the question remains open will still have an undiminished incentive to litigate the issue. This Court can then grant certiorari, and the development of Fourth Amendment law will in no way be stunted.

Davis argues that Fourth Amendment precedents of *this* Court will be effectively insulated from challenge under a good-faith exception for reliance on appellate precedent. But this argument is overblown. For one thing, it is important to keep in mind that this argument applies to an exceedingly small set of cases. Decisions overruling this Court's Fourth Amendment precedents are rare. Indeed, it has been more than 40 years since the Court last handed down a decision of the type to which Davis refers. Chimel v. California, 395 U.S. 752 (1969) (overruling United States v. Rabinowitz, 339 U.S. 56 (1950), and Harris v. United States, 331 U.S. 145 (1947)). And even in those cases, Davis points out that no fewer than eight separate doctrines may preclude a defendant who successfully challenges an existing precedent from getting any relief. Moreover, as a practical matter, defense counsel in many cases will test this Court's Fourth Amendment precedents in the same way that *Belton* was tested in *Gant*—by arguing that the precedent is distinguishable.

At most, Davis's argument might suggest that—to prevent Fourth Amendment law from becoming ossified—the petitioner in a case that results in the overruling of one of this Court's Fourth Amendment precedents should be given the benefit of the victory by permitting the suppression of evidence in that one case. Such a result would undoubtedly be a windfall to this one random litigant. But the exclusionary rule is not a personal constitutional right. It is a judicially created sanction, specifically designed as a "windfall" remedy to deter future Fourth Amendment violations. The good-faith exception is a judicially created exception to this judicially created rule. Therefore, in a future case, we could, if necessary, recognize a limited exception to the good-faith exception for a defendant who obtains a judgment over-ruling one of our Fourth Amendment precedents. But this is not such a case. Davis did not secure a decision overturning a Supreme Court precedent; the police in his case reasonably relied on binding Circuit precedent. ...

It is one thing for the criminal "to go free because the constable has blundered." People v. Defore, 150 N.E. 585, 587 (N.Y. 1926) (Cardozo, J.). It is quite another to set the criminal free because the constable has scrupulously adhered to governing law. Excluding evidence in such cases deters no police misconduct and imposes substantial social costs. We therefore hold that when the police conduct a search in objectively reasonable reliance on binding appellate precedent, the exclusionary rule does not apply....

SOTOMAYOR, J., concurring in the judgment.

Under our precedents, the primary purpose of the exclusionary rule is to deter future Fourth Amendment violations. Accordingly, we have held, application of the exclusionary rule is unwarranted when it does not result in appreciable deterrence. In the circumstances of this case, where binding appellate precedent specifically *authorized* a particular police practice, in accord with the holdings of nearly every other court in the country—application of the exclusionary rule cannot reasonably be expected to yield appreciable deterrence. I am thus compelled to conclude that the exclusionary rule does not apply in this case and to agree with the Court's disposition.

This case does not present the markedly different question whether the exclusionary rule applies when the law governing the constitutionality of a particular search is unsettled.... The Court of Appeals recognized as much in limiting its application of the good-faith exception it articulated in this case to situations where its precedent on a given point is "unequivocal." 598 F.3d at 1266; see *id.,* at 1266–1267 ("[We] do not mean to encourage police to adopt a 'let's-wait-until-it's-decided approach' to unsettled questions of Fourth Amendment law"). Whether exclusion would deter Fourth Amendment violations where appellate precedent does not specifically authorize a certain practice and, if so, whether the benefits of exclusion would outweigh its costs are questions unanswered by our previous decisions.

The dissent suggests that today's decision essentially answers those questions, noting that an officer who conducts a search in the face of unsettled precedent "is no more culpable than an officer who follows erroneous binding precedent." The Court does not address this issue. In my view, whether an officer's conduct can be characterized as "culpable" is not itself dispositive. We have never refused to apply the exclusionary rule where its application would appreciably deter Fourth Amendment violations on the mere ground that the officer's conduct could be characterized as nonculpable. Rather, an officer's culpability is relevant because it may inform the overarching inquiry whether exclusion would result in appreciable deterrence. Whatever we have said about culpability, the ultimate questions have always been, one, whether exclusion would result in appreciable deterrence and, two, whether the benefits of exclusion outweigh its costs.

As stated, whether exclusion would result in appreciable deterrence in the circumstances of this case is a different question from whether exclusion would appreciably deter Fourth Amendment violations when the governing law is unsettled. The Court's answer to the former question in this case thus does not resolve the latter one.

BREYER, J., dissenting.[*]

In 2009, in Arizona v. Gant, this Court held that a police search of an automobile without a warrant violates the Fourth Amendment if the police have previously removed the automobile's occupants and placed them securely in a squad car. The present case involves these same circumstances, and it was pending on appeal when this Court decided *Gant.* Because *Gant* represents a "shift" in the Court's Fourth Amendment jurisprudence, we must decide *whether* and *how Gant's* new rule applies here.

I

I agree with the Court about *whether Gant's* new rule applies. It does apply. Between 1965 and 1987, [after the Court decided *Linkletter* and before it decided *Griffith*], that conclusion would have been more difficult to reach. Under *Linkletter,* the Court determined a new rule's retroactivity by looking to several different factors, including whether the

---

[*] Justice Ginsburg joined this opinion.

new rule represented a "clear break" with the past and the degree of "reliance by law enforcement authorities on the old standards." And the Court would often not apply the new rule to identical cases still pending on appeal.

After 22 years of struggling with its *Linkletter* approach, however, the Court decided in *Griffith* that *Linkletter* had proved unfair and unworkable. It then substituted a clearer approach, stating that "a new rule for the conduct of criminal prosecutions is to be applied retroactively to all cases, state or federal, pending on direct review or not yet final, with no exception for cases in which the new rule constitutes a 'clear break' with the past." 479 U.S., at 328. The Court today, following *Griffith,* concludes that *Gant'* s new rule applies here. And to that extent I agree with its decision.

II

The Court goes on, however, to decide *how Gant's* new rule will apply. And here it adds a fatal twist. While conceding that, like the search in *Gant,* this search violated the Fourth Amendment, it holds that, unlike Gant, this defendant is not entitled to a remedy. That is because the Court finds a new "good faith" exception which prevents application of the normal remedy for a Fourth Amendment violation, namely, suppression of the illegally seized evidence. Leaving Davis with a right but not a remedy, the Court "keep[s] the word of promise to our ear" but "break[s] it to our hope."

A

At this point I can no longer agree with the Court. A new "good faith" exception and this Court's retroactivity decisions are incompatible. For one thing, the Court's distinction between (1) retroactive application of a new rule and (2) availability of a remedy is highly artificial and runs counter to precedent. To determine that a new rule is retroactive *is* to determine that, at least in the normal case, there is a remedy. As we have previously said, the source of a "new rule" is the Constitution itself, not any judicial power to create new rules of law; hence, what we are actually determining when we assess the "retroactivity" of a new rule is not the temporal scope of a newly announced right, but whether a violation of the right that occurred prior to the announcement of the new rule will entitle a criminal defendant to the relief sought. The Court's "good faith" exception (unlike, say, inevitable discovery, a remedial doctrine that applies only upon occasion) creates "a categorical bar to obtaining redress" in *every* case pending when a precedent is overturned.

For another thing, the Court's holding re-creates the very problems that led the Court to abandon *Linkletter*'s approach to retroactivity in favor of *Griffith*'s. One such problem concerns workability. The Court says that its exception applies where there is "objectively reasonable" police "reliance on binding appellate precedent." But to apply the term "binding appellate precedent" often requires resolution of complex questions of degree. Davis conceded that he faced binding anti-*Gant* precedent in the Eleventh Circuit. But future litigants will be less forthcoming. Indeed, those litigants will now have to create distinctions to show that previous Circuit precedent was not "binding" lest they find relief foreclosed even if they win their constitutional claim.

At the same time, Fourth Amendment precedents frequently require courts to "slosh" their way through the factbound morass of "reasonableness." Scott v. Harris, 550 U.S. 372, 383 (2007). Suppose an officer's conduct is consistent with the language of a Fourth Amendment rule that a court of appeals announced in a case with clearly distinguishable facts? Suppose the case creating the relevant precedent did not directly announce any general rule but involved highly analogous facts? What about a rule that all other jurisdictions, but not the defendant's jurisdiction, had previously accepted? What rules can be developed for determining when, where, and how these different kinds of precedents do, or do not, count as relevant "binding precedent"? The *Linkletter*-like result is likely complex legal argument and police force confusion.

Another such problem concerns fairness. Today's holding, like that in *Linkletter,* violates basic norms of constitutional adjudication. It treats the defendant in a case announcing a new rule one way while treating similarly situated defendants whose cases are pending on appeal in a different way. …

Of course, the Court may, as it suggests, avoid this unfairness by refusing to apply the exclusionary rule even to the defendant in the very case in which it announces a "new rule." But that approach would make matters worse. What would then happen in the lower courts? How would courts of appeals, for example, come to reconsider their prior decisions when other circuits' cases lead them to believe those decisions may be wrong? Why would a defendant seek to overturn any such decision? After all, if the (incorrect) circuit precedent is clear, then even if the defendant wins (on the constitutional question), he loses (on relief). To what extent then could this Court rely upon lower courts to work out Fourth Amendment differences among themselves—through circuit reconsideration of a precedent that other circuits have criticized?

B

Perhaps more important, the Court's rationale for creating its new "good faith" exception threatens to undermine well-settled Fourth Amendment law. The Court [reasons that the deterrence benefits] are sufficient to justify exclusion where "police exhibit deliberate, reckless, or grossly negligent disregard for Fourth Amendment rights." But those benefits do not justify exclusion where, as here, the police act with "simple, isolated negligence" or an "objectively reasonable good-faith belief that their conduct is lawful."

If the Court means what it says, what will happen to the exclusionary rule, a rule that the Court adopted nearly a century ago for federal courts, and made applicable to state courts a half century ago through the Fourteenth Amendment? The Court has thought of that rule not as punishment for the individual officer or as reparation for the individual defendant but more generally as an effective way to secure enforcement of the Fourth Amendment's commands. This Court has deviated from the "suppression" norm in the name of "good faith" only a handful of times and in limited, atypical circumstances: where a magistrate has erroneously issued a warrant, where a database has erroneously informed police that they have a warrant, and where an unconstitutional statute purported to authorize the search.

The fact that such exceptions are few and far between is understandable. Defendants frequently move to suppress evidence on Fourth Amendment grounds. In many, perhaps most, of these instances the police, uncertain of how the Fourth Amendment applied to the particular factual circumstances they faced, will have acted in objective good faith. Yet, in a significant percentage of these instances, courts will find that the police were wrong. And, unless the police conduct falls into one of the exceptions previously noted, courts have required the suppression of the evidence seized. See Valdes, Frequency and Success: An Empirical Study of Criminal Law Defenses, Federal Constitutional Evidentiary Claims, and Plea Negotiations, 153 U. Pa. L. Rev. 1709, 1728 (2005) (suppression motions are filed in approximately 7% of criminal cases; approximately 12% of suppression motions are successful).

But an officer who conducts a search that he believes complies with the Constitution but which, it ultimately turns out, falls just outside the Fourth Amendment's bounds is no more culpable than an officer who follows erroneous "binding precedent." Nor is an officer more culpable where circuit precedent is simply suggestive rather than "binding," where it only describes how to treat roughly analogous instances, or where it just does not exist. Thus, if the Court means what it now says, if it would place determinative weight upon the culpability of an individual officer's conduct, and if it would apply the exclusionary rule only where a Fourth Amendment violation was "deliberate, reckless, or grossly negligent," then the "good faith" exception will swallow the exclusionary rule. Indeed, our broad dicta in *Herring*—dicta the Court repeats and expands upon today—may already be leading lower courts in this direction. Today's decision will doubtless accelerate this trend. ...

2. Causation Limits: Inevitable Discovery and Independent Source

Page 422. Add this material at the end of note 5.

See also Wilder v. State, 717 S.E.2d 457 (Ga. 2011) (initial warrantless seizure of briefcase during child molestation investigation, followed by warranted search of briefcase based on same information used to justify seizure; independent source exception not available).

C. Additions and Alternatives to the Exclusionary Rule

1. Administrative Remedies

Page 437. Add this new note after note 6.

7. *Non-constitutional "law of policing."* Professor Rachel Harmon, in her article, "The Problem of Policing," 110 Mich. L. Rev. 761 (2012), calls attention to the role of non-judicial local, state and federal institutions – particularly the role of civil service law, collective bargaining law, and federal and state employment discrimination law – in creating a regulatory regime for police, not limited to constitutional boundaries. Cf. Claremont Police Officers Ass'n v. City of Claremont,

139 P.3d 532 (Cal. 2006) (police association resisted implementation of racial profiling policy as violation of collective bargaining agreement).

2. Tort Actions and Criminal Prosecutions

Page 449. Add this material before the notes.

Problem 6-5A. Checking with the Boss

Shelly Kelly decided to break off her romantic relationship with Jerry Ray Bowen and move out of her apartment, to which Bowen had a key. Bowen had assaulted Kelly in the past and had been convicted of several violent felonies. She therefore asked officers from the Los Angeles County Sheriff's Department to accompany her while she gathered her things from the apartment. Deputies from the Sheriff's Department came to assist Kelly but were called away to respond to an emergency before the move was complete.

As soon as the officers left, an enraged Bowen appeared at the bottom of the stairs to the apartment, yelling "I told you never to call the cops on me bitch!" Bowen then ran up the stairs to Kelly and tried to throw her over the railing of the second-story landing. Kelly managed to escape and ran to her car. By that time, Bowen had retrieved a black sawed-off shotgun with a pistol grip. He ran in front of Kelly's car, pointed the shotgun at her, and told Kelly that if she tried to leave he would kill her. Kelly sped away, while Bowen fired at the car five times, blowing out the car's left front tire in the process.

Kelly quickly located police officers and reported the assault. She told Detective Curt Messerschmidt about Bowen's assault that day, his previous assaults on her, and mentioned that he was an active member of the "Mona Park Crips," a local street gang. Kelly said that she thought Bowen was staying at the home of his former foster mother, Augusta Millender.

Based on a search of governmental records, Messerschmidt confirmed that Bowen had some current connection to Millender's home, that he was an active gang member, and that he had been arrested and convicted for numerous violent and firearm-related offenses. On this basis, Messerschmidt prepared a warrant to authorize the search of Millender's house. An attachment to the search warrant described the property that would be the object of the search:

> All handguns, rifles, or shotguns of any caliber, or any firearms
> capable of firing ammunition, or firearms or devices modified or
> designed to allow it [*sic*] to fire ammunition. All caliber of
> ammunition, miscellaneous gun parts, gun cleaning kits, holsters
> which could hold or have held any caliber handgun being sought.
> Any receipts or paperwork, showing the purchase, ownership, or
> possession of the handguns being sought. Any firearm for which there
> is no proof of ownership. Any firearm capable of firing or chambered
> to fire any caliber ammunition.
>   Articles of evidence showing street gang membership or
> affiliation with any Street Gang to include but not limited to any
> reference to "Mona Park Crips", including writings or graffiti
> depicting gang membership, activity or identity. Articles of personal
> property tending to establish the identity of person [*sic*] in control of
> the premise or premises. Any photographs or photograph albums
> depicting persons, vehicles, weapons or locations, which may appear
> relevant to gang membership, or which may depict the item being
> sought and or believed to be evidence in the case being investigated
> on this warrant, or which may depict evidence of criminal activity.
> Additionally to include any gang indicia that would establish the
> persons being sought in this warrant, affiliation or membership with
> the "Mona Park Crips" street gang.

Two affidavits accompanied Messerschmidt's warrant application.
The first affidavit described Messerschmidt's extensive law enforcement
experience, including that he had served as a peace officer for 14 years,
that he was then assigned to a specialized unit investigating gang related
crimes, that he had been involved in "hundreds of gang related incidents,
contacts, and or arrests" during his time on the force, and that he had
"received specialized training in the field of gang related crimes" and
training in "gang related shootings."

The second affidavit explained why Messerschmidt believed there
was sufficient probable cause to support the warrant. That affidavit
described the facts of the incident involving Kelly and Bowen in great
detail, including the weapon used in the assault. It described the crime as
a "domestic assault." The affidavit also reported that a background check
based on governmental records gave Messerschmidt reason to believe
that Bowen resided at Millender's home. The affidavit requested that the
search warrant be endorsed for night service because Bowen had ties to
the Mona Park Crip gang and that "night service would provide an added

element of safety to the community as well as for the deputy personnel serving the warrant."

Messerschmidt submitted the warrants to two supervisors at the police department for review. A Deputy District Attorney also reviewed the materials and initialed the search warrant, indicating that she agreed with Messerschmidt's assessment of probable cause. At that point, Messerschmidt submitted the warrants to a magistrate, who approved the warrants and authorized night service.

The search warrant was served two days later by a team of officers. Sheriff's deputies forced open the front door and encountered Augusta Millender—a woman in her seventies—and Millender's daughter and grandson. All three of them lived in the home, along with seven other sporadic residents, including Bowen. The Millenders went outside while the residence was secured but remained in the living room while the search was conducted. Officers did not find Bowen in the residence. The search resulted in the seizure of Augusta Millender's shotgun, a letter addressed to Bowen from a state social services agency, and a box of .45–caliber ammunition.

If Millender files a tort suit against the Sheriff's Department and Messerschmidt for an invasion of property and privacy, will she obtain a favorable judgment, despite immunity doctrines? Will Millender collect any damages? Cf. Messerschmidt v. Millender, 132 S. Ct. 1235 (2012).

Page 450. Add this material at the end of note 3.

In Messerschmidt v. Millender, 132 S. Ct. 1235 (2012), the Court stressed that qualified immunity would be available to officers who act in reliance on a search warrant in all but the most unusual cases. The Court also concluded (for the first time, according to the dissent) that the detective's efforts to get supervisor and prosecutor approval for his warrant application before submitting it to the magistrate added further weight to his case for qualified immunity.

Page 452. Add this material at the end of note 8.

See Mary Fan, Panopticism for Police: Structural Reform Bargaining and Police Regulation by Data-Driven Surveillance, 87 Wash. L. Rev. 93 (2012) (remedies fashioned in shadow of threatened civil litigation can concentrate on data collection and access for greatest impact).

Chapter 7
Technology and Privacy

A. Enhancement of the Senses

Page 464. Add this material before Problem 7-1.

What is the relevance of eighteenth century text to twenty-first century technologies? For every new technology that police use to seize or search objects or individuals, courts must wrestle with this puzzle. This was true in the early twentieth century with wiretaps, and then later with bugs, beepers, pen registers (how quaint), cell phones and computers.

Early in the twenty-first century new twists on this puzzle have arisen with fairly specialized technology like forward-looking infra-red radar (discussed in Kyllo v. United States, 533 U.S. 27 (2001)), and with the increasingly common devices like GPS.

The following case, United States v. Jones, is both the most recent major United States Supreme Court decision applying the Fourth Amendment to a new technology, and a quirky technological remnant since the government relied on the use of a government-planted GPS tracking device rather than making use of the GPS and location identifiers built into cell phones, cars, and other pervasive contemporary devices.

Jones is a fascinating case doctrinally: while the court unanimously finds that the use of the GPS in this instance was an unconstitutional search, pay special attention to the role of *Katz* in determining whether a search occurred. But it is also a fascinating case for what it suggests and asks about institutional competence to respond to a changing balance of power between the state and individuals—and between private actors—and changing capacities for maintaining or invading privacy.

United States v. Antoine Jones
132 S. Ct. 945 (2012)

SCALIA, J.[*]

We decide whether the attachment of a Global-Positioning-System (GPS) tracking device to an individual's vehicle, and subsequent use of that device to monitor the vehicle's movements on public streets, constitutes a search or seizure within the meaning of the Fourth Amendment.

I

In 2004 respondent Antoine Jones, owner and operator of a nightclub in the District of Columbia, came under suspicion of trafficking in narcotics and was made the target of an investigation by a joint FBI and Metropolitan Police Department task force. Officers employed various investigative techniques, including visual surveillance of the nightclub, installation of a camera focused on the front door of the club, and a pen register and wiretap covering Jones's cellular phone.

Based in part on information gathered from these sources, in 2005 the Government applied to the United States District Court for the District of Columbia for a warrant authorizing the use of an electronic tracking device on the Jeep Grand Cherokee registered to Jones's wife. A warrant issued, authorizing installation of the device in the District of Columbia and within 10 days.

On the 11th day, and not in the District of Columbia but in Maryland, agents installed a GPS tracking device on the undercarriage of the Jeep while it was parked in a public parking lot. Over the next 28 days, the Government used the device to track the vehicle's movements, and once had to replace the device's battery when the vehicle was parked in a different public lot in Maryland. By means of signals from multiple satellites, the device established the vehicle's location within 50 to 100 feet, and communicated that location by cellular phone to a Government computer. It relayed more than 2,000 pages of data over the 4-week period.

---

[*] Chief Justice Roberts and Justices Kennedy, Thomas, and Sotomayor joined this opinion. – EDS.

The Government ultimately obtained a multiple-count indictment charging Jones and several alleged co-conspirators with … conspiracy to distribute and possess with intent to distribute five kilograms or more of cocaine and 50 grams or more of cocaine base…. Before trial, Jones filed a motion to suppress evidence obtained through the GPS device. The District Court granted the motion only in part, suppressing the data obtained while the vehicle was parked in the garage adjoining Jones's residence. It held the remaining data admissible, because "a person traveling in an automobile on public thoroughfares has no reasonable expectation of privacy in his movements from one place to another." Jones's trial in October 2006 produced a hung jury on the conspiracy count.

In March 2007, a grand jury returned another indictment, charging Jones and others with the same conspiracy. The Government introduced at trial the same GPS-derived locational data admitted in the first trial, which connected Jones to the alleged conspirators' stash house that contained $850,000 in cash, 97 kilograms of cocaine, and 1 kilogram of cocaine base. The jury returned a guilty verdict, and the District Court sentenced Jones to life imprisonment….

II A

The Fourth Amendment provides in relevant part that the "right of the people to be secure in their persons, houses, papers, and effects, against unreasonable searches and seizures, shall not be violated." It is beyond dispute that a vehicle is an "effect" as that term is used in the Amendment. We hold that the Government's installation of a GPS device on a target's vehicle,[2] and its use of that device to monitor the vehicle's movements, constitutes a "search."

It is important to be clear about what occurred in this case: The Government physically occupied private property for the purpose of obtaining information. We have no doubt that such a physical intrusion would have been considered a "search" within the meaning of the Fourth Amendment when it was adopted. Entick v. Carrington, 95 Eng. Rep. 807 (C.P. 1765), is a case we have described as a "monument of English

---

[2] [The] Jeep was registered to Jones's wife. The Government acknowledged, however, that Jones was the exclusive driver. If Jones was not the owner he had at least the property rights of a bailee. The Court of Appeals concluded that the vehicle's registration did not affect his ability to make a Fourth Amendment objection, and the Government has not challenged that determination here. We therefore do not consider the Fourth Amendment significance of Jones's status.

freedom" undoubtedly familiar to "every American statesman" at the time the Constitution was adopted, and considered to be "the true and ultimate expression of constitutional law" with regard to search and seizure. In that case, Lord Camden expressed in plain terms the significance of property rights in search-and-seizure analysis:

> [Our] law holds the property of every man so sacred, that no man can set his foot upon his neighbour's close without his leave; if he does he is a trespasser, though he does no damage at all; if he will tread upon his neighbour's ground, he must justify it by law.

The text of the Fourth Amendment reflects its close connection to property, since otherwise it would have referred simply to "the right of the people to be secure against unreasonable searches and seizures"; the phrase "in their persons, houses, papers, and effects" would have been superfluous.

Consistent with this understanding, our Fourth Amendment jurisprudence was tied to common-law trespass, at least until the latter half of the 20th century. Thus, in Olmstead v. United States, 277 U.S. 438 (1928), we held that wiretaps attached to telephone wires on the public streets did not constitute a Fourth Amendment search because there was "no entry of the houses or offices of the defendants."

Our later cases, of course, have deviated from that exclusively property-based approach. In Katz v. United States, 389 U.S. 347 (1967), we said that "the Fourth Amendment protects people, not places," and found a violation in attachment of an eavesdropping device to a public telephone booth. Our later cases have applied the analysis of Justice Harlan's concurrence in that case, which said that a violation occurs when government officers violate a person's "reasonable expectation of privacy." See, e.g., Bond v. United States, 529 U.S. 334 (2000).

The Government contends that the Harlan standard shows that no search occurred here, since Jones had no "reasonable expectation of privacy" in the area of the Jeep accessed by Government agents (its underbody) and in the locations of the Jeep on the public roads, which were visible to all. But we need not address the Government's contentions, because Jones's Fourth Amendment rights do not rise or fall with the Katz formulation. At bottom, we must assure preservation of that degree of privacy against government that existed when the Fourth Amendment was adopted. As explained, for most of our history the Fourth Amendment was understood to embody a particular concern for government trespass upon the areas ("persons, houses, papers, and effects") it enumerates.[3] *Katz* did not repudiate that understanding. Less than two years later the Court upheld defendants' contention that the Government could not introduce against them conversations between *other* people obtained by warrantless placement of electronic surveillance devices in their homes. The opinion rejected the dissent's contention that there was no Fourth Amendment violation "unless the conversational privacy of the homeowner himself is invaded." Alderman v. United States, 394 U.S. 165 (1969). "[We do not] believe that *Katz,* by holding that the Fourth Amendment protects persons and their private conversations, was intended to withdraw any of the protection which the Amendment extends to the home...." *Katz* did not narrow the Fourth Amendment's scope.[5]

The Government contends that several of our post-*Katz* cases foreclose the conclusion that what occurred here constituted a search. It relies principally on two cases in which we rejected Fourth Amendment

---

[3] Justice Alito's concurrence doubts the wisdom of our approach because "it is almost impossible to think of late–18th–century situations that are analogous to what took place in this case." But in fact it posits a situation that is not far afield—a constable's concealing himself in the target's coach in order to track its movements. There is no doubt that the information gained by that trespassory activity would be the product of an unlawful search—whether that information consisted of the conversations occurring in the coach, or of the destinations to which the coach traveled.

In any case, it is quite irrelevant whether there was an 18th-century analog. Whatever new methods of investigation may be devised, our task, *at a minimum,* is to decide whether the action in question would have constituted a "search" within the original meaning of the Fourth Amendment. Where, as here, the Government obtains information by physically intruding on a constitutionally protected area, such a search has undoubtedly occurred.

[5] The concurrence notes that post-*Katz* we have explained that "an actual trespass is neither necessary *nor sufficient* to establish a constitutional violation." That is undoubtedly true, and undoubtedly irrelevant. [The Court in United States v. Karo, 468 U.S. 705 (1984)] was considering whether a seizure occurred, and as the concurrence explains, a seizure of property occurs, not when there is a trespass, but "when there is some meaningful interference with an individual's possessory interests in that property." Likewise with a search. Trespass alone does not qualify, but there must be conjoined with that what was present here: an attempt to find something or to obtain information.

Related to this, and similarly irrelevant, is the concurrence's point that, if analyzed separately, neither the installation of the device nor its use would constitute a Fourth Amendment search. Of course not. A trespass on "houses" or "effects," or a *Katz* invasion of privacy, is not alone a search unless it is done to obtain information; and the obtaining of information is not alone a search unless it is achieved by such a trespass or invasion of privacy.

challenges to "beepers," electronic tracking devices that represent another form of electronic monitoring. The first case, United States v. Knotts, 460 U.S. 276 (1983), upheld against Fourth Amendment challenge the use of a "beeper" that had been placed in a container of chloroform, allowing law enforcement to monitor the location of the container. We said that there had been no infringement of Knotts' reasonable expectation of privacy since the information obtained—the location of the automobile carrying the container on public roads, and the location of the off-loaded container in open fields near Knotts' cabin— had been voluntarily conveyed to the public. But as we have discussed, the *Katz* reasonable-expectation-of-privacy test has been *added to,* not *substituted for,* the common-law trespassory test. The holding in *Knotts* addressed only the former, since the latter was not at issue. The beeper had been placed in the container before it came into Knotts' possession, with the consent of the then-owner. Knotts did not challenge that installation, and we specifically declined to consider its effect on the Fourth Amendment analysis. *Knotts* would be relevant, perhaps, if the Government were making the argument that what would otherwise be an unconstitutional search is not such where it produces only public information. The Government does not make that argument, and we know of no case that would support it.

The second "beeper" case, United States v. Karo, 468 U.S. 705 (1984), does not suggest a different conclusion. There we addressed the question left open by *Knotts,* whether the installation of a beeper in a container amounted to a search or seizure. As in *Knotts,* at the time the beeper was installed the container belonged to a third party, and it did not come into possession of the defendant until later. Thus, the specific question we considered was whether the installation "*with the consent of the original owner*" constituted a search or seizure "when the container is delivered to a buyer having no knowledge of the presence of the beeper." We held not.... Karo accepted the container as it came to him, beeper and all, and was therefore not entitled to object to the beeper's presence, even though it was used to monitor the container's location. Jones, who possessed the Jeep at the time the Government trespassorily inserted the information-gathering device, is on much different footing....

B

The concurrence begins by accusing us of applying "18th-century tort law." That is a distortion. What we apply is an 18th-century guarantee against unreasonable searches, which we believe must provide *at a minimum* the degree of protection it afforded when it was adopted. The concurrence does not share that belief. It would apply *exclusively* *Katz*'s reasonable-expectation-of-privacy test, even when that eliminates rights that previously existed.

The concurrence faults our approach for presenting "particularly vexing problems" in cases that do not involve physical contact, such as those that involve the transmission of electronic signals. We entirely fail to understand that point. For unlike the concurrence, which would make *Katz* the *exclusive* test, we do not make trespass the exclusive test. Situations involving merely the transmission of electronic signals without trespass would *remain* subject to *Katz* analysis.

In fact, it is the concurrence's insistence on the exclusivity of the *Katz* test that needlessly leads us into "particularly vexing problems" in the present case. This Court has to date not deviated from the understanding that mere visual observation does not constitute a search. We accordingly held in *Knotts* that a "person traveling in an automobile on public thoroughfares has no reasonable expectation of privacy in his movements from one place to another." Thus, even assuming that the concurrence is correct to say that "traditional surveillance" of Jones for a 4-week period "would have required a large team of agents, multiple vehicles, and perhaps aerial assistance," our cases suggest that such visual observation is constitutionally permissible. It may be that achieving the same result through electronic means, without an accompanying trespass, is an unconstitutional invasion of privacy, but the present case does not require us to answer that question.

And answering it affirmatively leads us needlessly into additional thorny problems. The concurrence posits that "relatively short-term monitoring of a person's movements on public streets" is okay, but that "the use of longer term GPS monitoring in investigations *of most offenses*" is no good. That introduces yet another novelty into our jurisprudence. There is no precedent for the proposition that whether a search has occurred depends on the nature of the crime being investigated. And even accepting that novelty, it remains unexplained why a 4-week investigation is "surely" too long and why a drug-trafficking conspiracy involving substantial amounts of cash and narcotics is not an "extraordinary" offense which may permit longer observation. What of a 2-day monitoring of a suspected purveyor of stolen electronics? Or of a 6–month monitoring of a suspected terrorist?

We may have to grapple with these "vexing problems" in some future case where a classic trespassory search is not involved and resort must be had to *Katz* analysis; but there is no reason for rushing forward to resolve them here....

SOTOMAYOR, J., concurring.

[The] Fourth Amendment is not concerned only with trespassory intrusions on property. Rather, even in the absence of a trespass, a Fourth Amendment search occurs when the government violates a subjective expectation of privacy that society recognizes as reasonable. In *Katz,* this Court enlarged its then-prevailing focus on property rights by announcing that the reach of the Fourth Amendment does not "turn upon the presence or absence of a physical intrusion." As the majority's opinion makes clear, however, *Katz*'s reasonable-expectation-of-privacy test augmented, but did not displace or diminish, the common-law trespassory test that preceded it....

Nonetheless, as Justice Alito notes, physical intrusion is now unnecessary to many forms of surveillance. With increasing regularity, the Government will be capable of duplicating the monitoring undertaken in this case by enlisting factory- or owner-installed vehicle tracking devices or GPS-enabled smartphones. In cases of electronic or other novel modes of surveillance that do not depend upon a physical invasion on property, the majority opinion's trespassory test may provide little guidance. But situations involving merely the transmission of electronic signals without trespass would *remain* subject to *Katz* analysis. As Justice Alito incisively observes, the same technological advances that have made possible nontrespassory surveillance techniques will also affect the *Katz* test by shaping the evolution of societal privacy expectations. Under that rubric, I agree with Justice Alito that, at the very least, "longer term GPS monitoring in investigations of most offenses impinges on expectations of privacy."

In cases involving even short-term monitoring, some unique attributes of GPS surveillance relevant to the *Katz* analysis will require particular attention. GPS monitoring generates a precise, comprehensive record of a person's public movements that reflects a wealth of detail about her familial, political, professional, religious, and sexual associations. See, e.g., People v. Weaver, 909 N.E.2d 1195 (N.Y. 2009) ("Disclosed in [GPS data] will be trips the indisputably private nature of which takes little imagination to conjure: trips to the psychiatrist, the plastic surgeon, the abortion clinic, the AIDS treatment center, the strip club, the criminal defense attorney, the by-the-hour motel, the union meeting, the mosque, synagogue or church, the gay bar and on and on"). The Government can store such records and efficiently mine them for information years into the future. And because GPS monitoring is cheap in comparison to conventional surveillance techniques and, by design, proceeds surreptitiously, it evades the ordinary checks that constrain abusive law enforcement practices: limited police resources and community hostility.

Awareness that the Government may be watching chills associational and expressive freedoms. And the Government's unrestrained power to assemble data that reveal private aspects of identity is susceptible to abuse. The net result is that GPS monitoring—by making available at a relatively low cost such a substantial quantum of intimate information about any person whom the Government, in its unfettered discretion, chooses to track—may alter the relationship between citizen and government in a way that is inimical to democratic society.

I would take these attributes of GPS monitoring into account when considering the existence of a reasonable societal expectation of privacy in the sum of one's public movements. I would ask whether people reasonably expect that their movements will be recorded and aggregated in a manner that enables the Government to ascertain, more or less at will, their political and religious beliefs, sexual habits, and so on. I do not regard as dispositive the fact that the Government might obtain the fruits of GPS monitoring through lawful conventional surveillance techniques. I would also consider the appropriateness of entrusting to the Executive, in the absence of any oversight from a coordinate branch, a tool so amenable to misuse, especially in light of the Fourth Amendment's goal to curb arbitrary exercises of police power to and prevent a too permeating police surveillance.

More fundamentally, it may be necessary to reconsider the premise that an individual has no reasonable expectation of privacy in information voluntarily disclosed to third parties. E.g., United States v. Miller, 425 U.S. 435 (1976). This approach is ill suited to the digital age, in which people reveal a great deal of information about themselves to third parties in the course of carrying out mundane tasks. People disclose the phone numbers that they dial or text to their cellular providers; the URLs that they visit and the e-mail addresses with which they correspond to their Internet service providers; and the books, groceries, and medications they purchase to online retailers. Perhaps, as Justice Alito notes, some people may find the "tradeoff" of privacy for convenience worthwhile, or come to accept this diminution of privacy as inevitable, and perhaps not. I for one doubt that people would accept without complaint the warrantless disclosure to the Government of a list of every Web site they had visited in the last week, or month, or year. But whatever the societal expectations, they can attain constitutionally protected status only if our Fourth Amendment jurisprudence ceases to treat secrecy as a prerequisite for privacy. I would not assume that all information voluntarily disclosed to some member of the public for a limited purpose is, for that reason alone, disentitled to Fourth Amendment protection....

Resolution of these difficult questions in this case is unnecessary, however, because the Government's physical intrusion on Jones' Jeep supplies a narrower basis for decision. I therefore join the majority's opinion.

ALITO, J., concurring in the judgment.[*]

This case requires us to apply the Fourth Amendment's prohibition of unreasonable searches and seizures to a 21st-century surveillance technique, the use of a Global Positioning System (GPS) device to monitor a vehicle's movements for an extended period of time. Ironically, the Court has chosen to decide this case based on 18th-century tort law. By attaching a small GPS device to the underside of the vehicle that respondent drove, the law enforcement officers in this case engaged in conduct that might have provided grounds in 1791 for a suit for trespass to chattels. And for this reason, the Court concludes, the installation and use of the GPS device constituted a search.

This holding, in my judgment, is unwise. It strains the language of the Fourth Amendment; it has little if any support in current Fourth Amendment case law; and it is highly artificial. I would analyze the question presented in this case by asking whether respondent's reasonable expectations of privacy were violated by the long-term monitoring of the movements of the vehicle he drove.

---

[*] Justices Ginsburg, Breyer, and Kagan joined this opinion. – EDS.

I

The Fourth Amendment prohibits "unreasonable searches and seizures," and the Court makes very little effort to explain how the attachment or use of the GPS device fits within these terms....

The Court argues—and I agree—that we must "assure preservation of that degree of privacy against government that existed when the Fourth Amendment was adopted." But it is almost impossible to think of late 18th-century situations that are analogous to what took place in this case.... The Court's theory seems to be that the concept of a search, as originally understood, comprehended any technical trespass that led to the gathering of evidence, but we know that this is incorrect. At common law, any unauthorized intrusion on private property was actionable, but a trespass on open fields, as opposed to the "curtilage" of a home, does not fall within the scope of the Fourth Amendment because private property outside the curtilage is not part of a "house" within the meaning of the Fourth Amendment. See Oliver v. United States, 466 U.S. 170 (1984).

The Court's reasoning in this case is very similar to that in the Court's early decisions involving wiretapping and electronic eavesdropping, namely, that a technical trespass followed by the gathering of evidence constitutes a search. In the early electronic surveillance cases, the Court concluded that a Fourth Amendment search occurred when private conversations were monitored as a result of an "unauthorized physical penetration into the premises occupied" by the defendant. Silverman v. United States, 365 U.S. 505 (1961). In *Silverman,* police officers listened to conversations in an attached home by inserting a "spike mike" through the wall that this house shared with the vacant house next door. This procedure was held to be a search because the mike made contact with a heating duct on the other side of the wall and thus "usurped ... an integral part of the premises."

By contrast, in cases in which there was no trespass, it was held that there was no search. Thus, in Olmstead v. United States, 277 U.S. 438 (1928), the Court found that the Fourth Amendment did not apply because the "taps from house lines were made in the streets near the houses." ...

This trespass-based rule was repeatedly criticized. In *Olmstead,* Justice Brandeis wrote that it was "immaterial where the physical connection with the telephone wires was made." Although a private conversation transmitted by wire did not fall within the literal words of the Fourth Amendment, he argued, the Amendment should be understood as prohibiting "every unjustifiable intrusion by the government upon the privacy of the individual."

Katz v. United States, 389 U.S. 347 (1967), finally did away with the old approach, holding that a trespass was not required for a Fourth Amendment violation. [The] *Katz* Court, repudiated the old doctrine and held that the fact that the "electronic device employed ... did not happen to penetrate the wall of the booth can have no constitutional significance." What mattered, the Court now held, was whether the conduct at issue "violated the privacy upon which [the defendant] justifiably relied while using the telephone booth." Under this approach, as the Court later put it when addressing the relevance of a technical trespass, "an actual trespass is neither necessary *nor sufficient* to establish a constitutional violation." United States v. Karo, 468 U.S. 705 (1984) (emphasis added). ...

III

[The] Court's reasoning largely disregards what is really important (the *use* of a GPS for the purpose of long-term tracking) and instead attaches great significance to something that most would view as relatively minor (attaching to the bottom of a car a small, light object that does not interfere in any way with the car's operation)....

[The] Court's reliance on the law of trespass will present particularly vexing problems in cases involving surveillance that is carried out by making electronic, as opposed to physical, contact with the item to be tracked. For example, suppose that the officers in the present case had followed respondent by surreptitiously activating a stolen vehicle detection system that came with the car when it was purchased....

IV

The *Katz* expectation-of-privacy test avoids the problems and complications noted above, but it is not without its own difficulties. It involves a degree of circularity, and judges are apt to confuse their own expectations of privacy with those of the hypothetical reasonable person to which the *Katz* test looks. In addition, the *Katz* test rests on the assumption that this hypothetical reasonable person has a well-developed and stable set of privacy expectations. But technology can change those expectations. Dramatic technological change may lead to periods in which popular expectations are in flux and may ultimately produce significant changes in popular attitudes. New technology may provide increased convenience or security at the expense of privacy, and many people may find the tradeoff worthwhile. And even if the public does not welcome the diminution of privacy that new technology entails, they may eventually reconcile themselves to this development as inevitable.

On the other hand, concern about new intrusions on privacy may spur the enactment of legislation to protect against these intrusions. This is what ultimately happened with respect to wiretapping. After *Katz,* Congress did not leave it to the courts to develop a body of Fourth Amendment case law governing that complex subject. Instead, Congress promptly enacted a comprehensive statute, see 18 U.S.C. §§ 2510–2522, and since that time, the regulation of wiretapping has been governed primarily by statute and not by case law. In an ironic sense, although *Katz* overruled *Olmstead,* Chief Justice Taft's suggestion in the latter case that the regulation of wiretapping was a matter better left for Congress, has been borne out.

Recent years have seen the emergence of many new devices that permit the monitoring of a person's movements. In some locales, closed-circuit television video monitoring is becoming ubiquitous. On toll roads, automatic toll collection systems create a precise record of the movements of motorists who choose to make use of that convenience. Many motorists purchase cars that are equipped with devices that permit a central station to ascertain the car's location at any time so that roadside assistance may be provided if needed and the car may be found if it is stolen.

Perhaps most significant, cell phones and other wireless devices now permit wireless carriers to track and record the location of users— and as of June 2011, it has been reported, there were more than 322 million wireless devices in use in the United States. For older phones, the accuracy of the location information depends on the density of the tower network, but new "smart phones," which are equipped with a GPS device, permit more precise tracking. For example, when a user activates the GPS on such a phone, a provider is able to monitor the phone's location and speed of movement and can then report back real-time traffic conditions after combining ("crowdsourcing") the speed of all such phones on any particular road. Similarly, phone-location-tracking services are offered as "social" tools, allowing consumers to find (or to avoid) others who enroll in these services. The availability and use of these and other new devices will continue to shape the average person's expectations about the privacy of his or her daily movements.

V

In the pre-computer age, the greatest protections of privacy were neither constitutional nor statutory, but practical. Traditional surveillance for any extended period of time was difficult and costly and therefore rarely undertaken. The surveillance at issue in this case—constant monitoring of the location of a vehicle for four weeks—would have required a large team of agents, multiple vehicles, and perhaps aerial assistance. Only an investigation of unusual importance could have justified such an expenditure of law enforcement resources. Devices like the one used in the present case, however, make long-term monitoring relatively easy and cheap. In circumstances involving dramatic technological change, the best solution to privacy concerns may be legislative. A legislative body is well situated to gauge changing public attitudes, to draw detailed lines, and to balance privacy and public safety in a comprehensive way.

To date, however, Congress and most States have not enacted statutes regulating the use of GPS tracking technology for law enforcement purposes. The best that we can do in this case is to apply existing Fourth Amendment doctrine and to ask whether the use of GPS tracking in a particular case involved a degree of intrusion that a reasonable person would not have anticipated.

Under this approach, relatively short-term monitoring of a person's movements on public streets accords with expectations of privacy that our society has recognized as reasonable. But the use of longer term GPS monitoring in investigations of most offenses impinges on expectations of privacy. For such offenses, society's expectation has been that law enforcement agents and others would not—and indeed, in the main, simply could not—secretly monitor and catalogue every single movement of an individual's car for a very long period. In this case, for four weeks, law enforcement agents tracked every movement that respondent made in the vehicle he was driving. We need not identify with precision the point at which the tracking of this vehicle became a search, for the line was surely crossed before the 4–week mark. Other cases may present more difficult questions. But where uncertainty exists with respect to whether a certain period of GPS surveillance is long enough to constitute a Fourth Amendment search, the police may always seek a warrant.[11] We also need not consider whether prolonged GPS monitoring in the context of investigations involving extraordinary offenses would similarly intrude on a constitutionally protected sphere of privacy. In such cases, long-term tracking might have been mounted using previously available techniques....

Notes

1. *Make it personal.* Consider the following exchange at oral argument in United States v. Jones. Michael Dreeben is a lawyer in the Solicitor General's Office of the United States Department of Justice.

> CHIEF JUSTICE ROBERTS: You think there would also not be a search if you put a GPS device on all of our cars, monitored our movements for a month? You think you're entitled to do that under your theory?
> MR. DREEBEN: The Justices of this Court?
> CHIEF JUSTICE ROBERTS: Yes. (Laughter.)
> MR. DREEBEN: Under our theory and under this Court's cases, the Justices of this Court when driving on public roadways have no greater expectation of —
> CHIEF JUSTICE ROBERTS: So, your answer is yes, you could tomorrow decide that you put a GPS device on every one of our cars, follow us for a month; no problem under the Constitution?
> MR. DREEBEN: Well, equally, Mr. Chief Justice, if the FBI wanted to, it could put a team of surveillance agents around the clock on any individual and follow that individual's movements as they went around on the public streets...

2. *Something old, something new. Entick* is a wonderful historical decision. But it had been cited by the Supreme only twice in this century, in Thornton v. United States, 541 U.S. 615 (2004) (search incident to arrest in vehicles), and in Kyllo v. United States, 533 U.S. 27 (2001)

---

[11] In this case, the agents obtained a warrant, but they did not comply with two of the warrant's restrictions: They did not install the GPS device within the 10–day period required by the terms of the warrant and by Fed. Rule Crim. Proc. 41(e)(2)(B)(i), and they did not install the GPS device within the District of Columbia, as required by the terms of the warrant and by 18 U.S.C. § 3117(a) and Rule 41(b)(4). In the courts below the Government did not argue, and has not argued here, that the Fourth Amendment does not impose these precise restrictions and that the violation of these restrictions does not demand the suppression of evidence obtained using the tracking device. Because it was not raised, that question is not before us.

(infra-red radar and homes). So why cite *Entick* again in *Jones*, with regard to GPS devices, of all things—unknown to repressive eighteenth century English authorities?

The side-stepping of *Katz* by the majority is a surprising development, as 44 years and countless citations attest. The significance of the doctrinal trespass "move" in assessing whether a search has occurred under the Fourth Amendment will on be apparent only over time. As the five concurring justices note, the relevance of physical trespass to searches using technology may be quite limited. The holding in this case may matter less over time than the larger issues about the challenges of technology to the Fourth Amendment and the questions about which institution is best positioned to respond to such developments. Justice Alito's rather uncharacteristic doctrinal suggestion that a complex balancing test under *Katz* should decide when the use of an attached GPS device is a search is balanced by his strong and perhaps compelling observation that courts are poorly situated either to weigh the values that should govern the uses of technology, or to regulate technologies.

Page 474. Add this material at the end of note 1.

See also People v. Bartelt, 948 N.E.2d 52 (Ill. 2011) (no "search" occurred when police dog's handler instructed stopped motorist to switch her ignition to auxiliary electricity, roll up the windows, and turn the ventilation system to high to exhaust the air from her truck; after this "set-up procedure," the dog alerted to the truck, and a search turned up evidence).

C. Records in the Hands of Third Parties

Page 511. Add this material at the end of note 2.

Compare State v. Mello, 27 A.3d 771 (N.H. 2011) (while there may be a reasonable expectation of privacy in the contents of internet communications, there is none in information voluntarily disclosed to a service provider to open an account); State v. Reid, 954 A.2d 503 (N.J. 2008) (state constitution provides customers of internet service providers a reasonable expectation of privacy in their subscriber information).

Chapter 8

Interrogations

A. *Voluntariness of Confessions*

2. Promises and Threats

Page 533. Add this material at the end of note 1.

See also State v. Hernandez, 34 A.3d 669 (N.H. 2011) (outright promise of confidentiality would render confession involuntary under state constitution, but confession here remained voluntary despite implied promise of confidentiality by interrogator, "Between you and me, ... the three of us in this room, OK, inside, inside your heart ... did you want to run [those people] over?"); Stanton v. Commonwealth, 349 S.W.3d 914 (Ky. 2011) (police officer and state social worker visited man suspected of sexually abusing his 12-year-old stepson; when he refused to go to stationhouse, social worker told him that children are removed from homes when allegations of sexual abuse raise reasonable concerns about safety of others; statement did not amount to a threat to remove child from home for non-cooperation with interrogation); Hill v. State, 12 A.3d 1193 (Md. 2011) (police officer's statement to suspect that victim of alleged crime did not want him to get into trouble and only wanted an apology amounted to an improper inducement, making the incriminating statement involuntary).

B. Miranda *Warnings*

2. "Triggering" *Miranda* Warnings

Page 558. Add this material before *State v. Elmarr*.

Federal and state courts agree that the determination of whether a suspect is in custody requires an objective determination of whether a reasonable person in the suspect's position would believe they had been constrained in a manner akin to arrest. The seminal opinion is Berkemer v. McCarty, 468 U.S. 420 (1984), a framework embraced as well by state courts.

But as any student of torts knows—and virtually every law student in the United States has studied the law of torts—there is no sharp line between what is objective or subjective. Nor does saying a test is "objective" settle the extent to which an assessment should be conducted in light of a few factual categories or all the particular facts of the case. As with the infinitely pliable concept of the reasonable person, the choice between simple categories and more contextual determination echoes throughout the law in battles over using more precise rules versus more flexible standards. These grand battles are illustrated in the following cases.

J.D.B. v. North Carolina
131 S. Ct. 2394 (2011)

SOTOMAYOR, J.[*]

This case presents the question whether the age of a child subjected to police questioning is relevant to the custody analysis of Miranda v. Arizona, 384 U.S. 436 (1966). It is beyond dispute that children will often feel bound to submit to police questioning when an adult in the same circumstances would feel free to leave. Seeing no reason for police officers or courts to blind themselves to that commonsense reality, we hold that a child's age properly informs the *Miranda* custody analysis.

---

[*] Justices Kennedy, Ginsburg, Breyer and Kagan joined this opinion.

I

... Petitioner J.D.B. was a 13-year-old, seventh-grade student attending class at Smith Middle School in Chapel Hill, North Carolina when he was removed from his classroom by a uniformed police officer, escorted to a closed-door conference room, and questioned by police for at least half an hour.

This was the second time that police questioned J.D.B. in the span of a week. Five days earlier, two home break-ins occurred, and various items were stolen. Police stopped and questioned J.D.B. after he was seen behind a residence in the neighborhood where the crimes occurred. That same day, police also spoke to J.D.B.'s grandmother—his legal guardian—as well as his aunt.

Police later learned that a digital camera matching the description of one of the stolen items had been found at J.D.B.'s middle school and seen in J.D.B.'s possession. Investigator DiCostanzo, the juvenile investigator with the local police force who had been assigned to the case, went to the school to question J.D.B. Upon arrival, DiCostanzo informed the uniformed police officer on detail to the school (a so-called school resource officer), the assistant principal, and an administrative intern that he was there to question J.D.B. about the break-ins. Although DiCostanzo asked the school administrators to verify J.D.B.'s date of birth, address, and parent contact information from school records, neither the police officers nor the school administrators contacted J.D.B.'s grandmother.

The uniformed officer interrupted J.D.B.'s afternoon social studies class, removed J.D.B. from the classroom, and escorted him to a school conference room. There, J.D.B. was met by DiCostanzo, the assistant principal, and the administrative intern. The door to the conference room was closed. With the two police officers and the two administrators present, J.D.B. was questioned for the next 30 to 45 minutes. Prior to the commencement of questioning, J.D.B. was given neither *Miranda* warnings nor the opportunity to speak to his grandmother. Nor was he informed that he was free to leave the room.

Questioning began with small talk—discussion of sports and J.D.B.'s family life. DiCostanzo asked, and J.D.B. agreed, to discuss the events of the prior weekend. Denying any wrongdoing, J.D.B. explained that he had been in the neighborhood where the crimes occurred because he was seeking work mowing lawns. DiCostanzo pressed J.D.B. for additional detail about his efforts to obtain work; asked J.D.B. to explain a prior incident, when one of the victims returned home to find J.D.B. behind her house; and confronted J.D.B. with the stolen camera. The assistant principal urged J.D.B. to "do the right thing," warning J.D.B. that "the truth always comes out in the end."

Eventually, J.D.B. asked whether he would "still be in trouble" if he returned the "stuff." In response, DiCostanzo explained that return of the stolen items would be helpful, but "this thing is going to court" regardless. ("What's done is done; now you need to help yourself by making it right"). DiCostanzo then warned that he may need to seek a secure custody order if he believed that J.D.B. would continue to break into other homes. When J.D.B. asked what a secure custody order was, DiCostanzo explained that "it's where you get sent to juvenile detention before court."

After learning of the prospect of juvenile detention, J.D.B. confessed that he and a friend were responsible for the break-ins. DiCostanzo only then informed J.D.B. that he could refuse to answer the investigator's questions and that he was free to leave. Asked whether he understood, J.D.B. nodded and provided further detail, including information about the location of the stolen items. Eventually J.D.B. wrote a statement, at DiCostanzo's request. When the bell rang indicating the end of the schoolday, J.D.B. was allowed to leave to catch the bus home....

Two juvenile petitions were filed against J.D.B., each alleging one count of breaking and entering and one count of larceny. J.D.B.'s public defender moved to suppress his statements and the evidence derived therefrom, arguing that suppression was necessary because J.D.B. had been interrogated by police in a custodial setting without being afforded *Miranda* warnings, and because his statements were involuntary under the totality of the circumstances test. After a suppression hearing at which DiCostanzo and J.D.B. testified, the trial court denied the motion, deciding that J.D.B. was not in custody at the time of the schoolhouse interrogation and that his statements were voluntary. As a result, J.D.B. entered a transcript of admission to all four counts, renewing his objection to the denial of his motion to suppress, and the court adjudicated J.D.B. delinquent. ... We granted certiorari to determine whether the *Miranda* custody analysis includes consideration of a juvenile suspect's age.

II A

Any police interview of an individual suspected of a crime has coercive aspects to it. Only those interrogations that occur while a suspect is in police custody, however, heighten the risk that statements obtained are not the product of the suspect's free choice.

By its very nature, custodial police interrogation entails inherently compelling pressures. Even for an adult, the physical and psychological isolation of custodial interrogation can undermine the individual's will to resist and compel him to speak where he would not otherwise do so freely. Indeed, the pressure of custodial interrogation is so immense that it "can induce a frighteningly high percentage of people to confess to crimes they never committed." Corley v. United States, 556 U.S. 303 (2009) (citing Drizin & Leo, The Problem of False Confessions in the Post–DNA World, 82 N.C. L. Rev. 891 (2004)). That risk is all the more troubling—and recent studies suggest, all the more acute—when the subject of custodial interrogation is a juvenile.

Recognizing that the inherently coercive nature of custodial interrogation "blurs the line between voluntary and involuntary statements," this Court in *Miranda* adopted a set of prophylactic measures designed to safeguard the constitutional guarantee against self-incrimination.... Because these measures protect the individual against the coercive nature of custodial interrogation, they are required only where there has been such a restriction on a person's freedom as to render him "in custody." As we have repeatedly emphasized, whether a suspect is "in custody" is an objective inquiry.

> Two discrete inquiries are essential to the determination: first, what were the circumstances surrounding the interrogation; and second, given those circumstances, would a reasonable person have felt he or she was at liberty to terminate the interrogation and leave. Once the scene is set and the players' lines and actions are reconstructed, the court must apply an objective test to resolve the ultimate inquiry: was there a formal arrest or restraint on freedom of movement of the degree associated with formal arrest.

Thompson v. Keohane, 516 U.S. 99, 112 (1995). Rather than demarcate a limited set of relevant circumstances, we have required police officers and courts to examine all of the circumstances surrounding the interrogation, including any circumstance that would have affected how a reasonable person in the suspect's position "would perceive his or her freedom to leave." Stansbury v. California, 511 U.S. 318, 325 (1994). On the other hand, the subjective views harbored by either the interrogating officers or the person being questioned are irrelevant. The test, in other words, involves no consideration of the actual mindset of the particular suspect subjected to police questioning.

The benefit of the objective custody analysis is that it is designed to give clear guidance to the police. Police must make in-the-moment judgments as to when to administer *Miranda* warnings. By limiting analysis to the objective circumstances of the interrogation, and asking how a reasonable person in the suspect's position would understand his freedom to terminate questioning and leave, the objective test avoids burdening police with the task of anticipating the idiosyncrasies of every individual suspect and divining how those particular traits affect each person's subjective state of mind.

B

The State and its *amici* contend that a child's age has no place in the custody analysis, no matter how young the child subjected to police questioning. We cannot agree. In some circumstances, a child's age would have affected how a "reasonable person" in the suspect's position would perceive his or her freedom to leave. That is, a reasonable child subjected to police questioning will sometimes feel pressured to submit when a reasonable adult would feel free to go. We think it clear that courts can account for that reality without doing any damage to the objective nature of the custody analysis.

A child's age is far more than a chronological fact. It is a fact that generates commonsense conclusions about behavior and perception. Such conclusions apply broadly to children as a class. And, they are self-evident to anyone who was a child once himself, including any police officer or judge.

Time and again, this Court has drawn these commonsense conclusions for itself. We have observed that children "generally are less mature and responsible than adults"; that they "often lack the experience, perspective, and judgment to recognize and avoid choices that could be detrimental to them"; that they "are more vulnerable or susceptible to ... outside pressures" than adults. Addressing the specific context of police interrogation, we have observed that events that "would leave a man cold and unimpressed can overawe and overwhelm a lad in his early teens." Haley v. Ohio, 332 U.S. 596 (1948) (plurality opinion). Describing no one child in particular, these observations restate what any parent knows—indeed, what any person knows—about children generally.[5]

Our various statements to this effect are far from unique. The law has historically reflected the same assumption that children characteristically lack the capacity to exercise mature judgment and possess only an incomplete ability to understand the world around them. See, *e.g.*, 1 W. Blackstone, Commentaries on the Laws of England *464–*465 (explaining that limits on children's legal capacity under the common law "secure them from hurting themselves by their own improvident acts"). Like this Court's own generalizations, the legal disqualifications placed on children as a class—*e.g.*, limitations on their ability to alienate property, enter a binding contract enforceable against them, and marry without parental consent—exhibit the settled understanding that the differentiating characteristics of youth are universal.

Indeed, even where a "reasonable person" standard otherwise applies, the common law has reflected the reality that children are not adults. In negligence suits, for instance, where liability turns on what an objectively reasonable person would do in the circumstances, "all American jurisdictions accept the idea that a person's childhood is a relevant circumstance" to be considered. Restatement (Third) of Torts §10, Comment *b*, p. 117 (2005).

As this discussion establishes, our history is replete with laws and judicial recognition that children cannot be viewed simply as miniature adults. We see no justification for taking a different course here. So long as the child's age was known to the officer at the time of the interview, or would have been objectively apparent to any reasonable officer, including age as part of the custody analysis requires officers neither to consider circumstances "unknowable" to them, nor to anticipate the frailties or idiosyncrasies of the particular suspect whom they question. The same "wide basis of community experience" that makes it possible, as an objective matter, "to determine what is to be expected" of children in other contexts, Restatement (Second) of Torts § 283A, at 15, likewise makes it possible to know what to expect of children subjected to police questioning.

In other words, a child's age differs from other personal

---

[5] Although citation to social science and cognitive science authorities is unnecessary to establish these commonsense propositions, the literature confirms what experience bears out. See, e.g., Graham v. Florida, 130 S. Ct. 2011, 2026 (2010) ("Developments in psychology and brain science continue to show fundamental differences between juvenile and adult minds").

characteristics that, even when known to police, have no objectively discernible relationship to a reasonable person's understanding of his freedom of action. Yarborough v. Alvarado, 541 U.S. 652 (2004), holds, for instance, that a suspect's prior interrogation history with law enforcement has no role to play in the custody analysis because such experience could just as easily lead a reasonable person to feel free to walk away as to feel compelled to stay in place. Because the effect in any given case would be contingent on the psychology of the individual suspect, the Court explained, such experience cannot be considered without compromising the objective nature of the custody analysis. A child's age, however, is different. Precisely because childhood yields objective conclusions like those we have drawn ourselves—among others, that children are "most susceptible to influence" and "outside pressures"—considering age in the custody analysis in no way involves a determination of how youth "subjectively affects the mindset" of any particular child.

In fact, in many cases involving juvenile suspects, the custody analysis would be nonsensical absent some consideration of the suspect's age. This case is a prime example. Were the court precluded from taking J.D.B.'s youth into account, it would be forced to evaluate the circumstances present here through the eyes of a reasonable person of average years. In other words, how would a reasonable adult understand his situation, after being removed from a seventh-grade social studies class by a uniformed school resource officer; being encouraged by his assistant principal to "do the right thing"; and being warned by a police investigator of the prospect of juvenile detention and separation from his guardian and primary caretaker? To describe such an inquiry is to demonstrate its absurdity. Neither officers nor courts can reasonably evaluate the effect of objective circumstances that, by their nature, are specific to children without accounting for the age of the child subjected to those circumstances.

Indeed, although the dissent suggests that concerns "regarding the application of the *Miranda* custody rule to minors can be accommodated by considering the unique circumstances present when minors are questioned in school," the effect of the schoolhouse setting cannot be disentangled from the identity of the person questioned. A student— whose presence at school is compulsory and whose disobedience at school is cause for disciplinary action—is in a far different position than, say, a parent volunteer on school grounds to chaperone an event, or an adult from the community on school grounds to attend a basketball game. Without asking whether the person questioned in school is a minor, the coercive effect of the schoolhouse setting is unknowable....

Reviewing the question *de novo* today, we hold that so long as the child's age was known to the officer at the time of police questioning, or would have been objectively apparent to a reasonable officer, its inclusion in the custody analysis is consistent with the objective nature of that test.[8] This is not to say that a child's age will be a determinative, or even a significant, factor in every case. It is, however, a reality that courts cannot simply ignore.

III

The State and its *amici* offer numerous reasons that courts must blind themselves to a juvenile defendant's age. None is persuasive....

Relying on our statements that the objective custody test is "designed to give clear guidance to the police," the State ... argues that a child's age must be excluded from the analysis in order to preserve clarity. Similarly, the dissent insists that the clarity of the custody analysis will be destroyed unless a "one-size-fits-all reasonable-person test" applies. In reality, however, ignoring a juvenile defendant's age will often make the inquiry more artificial, and thus only add confusion. And in any event, a child's age, when known or apparent, is hardly an obscure factor to assess. Though the State and the dissent worry about gradations among children of different ages, that concern cannot justify ignoring a child's age altogether. Just as police officers are competent to account for other objective circumstances that are a matter of degree such as the length of questioning or the number of officers present, so too are they competent to evaluate the effect of relative age. Indeed, they are competent to do so even though an interrogation room lacks the "reflective atmosphere" of a jury deliberation room. The same is true of judges, including those whose childhoods have long since passed. In short, officers and judges need no imaginative powers, knowledge of

---

[8] This approach does not undermine the basic principle that an interrogating officer's unarticulated, internal thoughts are never—in and of themselves—objective circumstances of an interrogation. Unlike a child's youth, an officer's purely internal thoughts have no conceivable effect on how a reasonable person in the suspect's position would understand his freedom of action. Rather than overturn that settled principle, the limitation that a child's age may inform the custody analysis only when known or knowable simply reflects our unwillingness to require officers to "make guesses" as to circumstances "unknowable" to them in deciding when to give *Miranda* warnings.

developmental psychology, training in cognitive science, or expertise in social and cultural anthropology to account for a child's age. They simply need the common sense to know that a 7–year–old is not a 13–year–old and neither is an adult.

There is, however, an even more fundamental flaw with the State's plea for clarity and the dissent's singular focus on simplifying the analysis: Not once have we excluded from the custody analysis a circumstance that we determined was relevant and objective, simply to make the fault line between custodial and noncustodial "brighter." Indeed, were the guiding concern clarity and nothing else, the custody test would presumably ask only whether the suspect had been placed under formal arrest. But we have rejected that "more easily administered line," recognizing that it would simply enable the police to circumvent the constraints on custodial interrogations established by *Miranda*....

Finally, the State and the dissent suggest that excluding age from the custody analysis comes at no cost to juveniles' constitutional rights because the due process voluntariness test independently accounts for a child's youth. To be sure, that test permits consideration of a child's age, and it erects its own barrier to admission of a defendant's inculpatory statements at trial. But *Miranda*'s procedural safeguards exist precisely because the voluntariness test is an inadequate barrier when custodial interrogation is at stake. To hold, as the State requests, that a child's age is never relevant to whether a suspect has been taken into custody—and thus to ignore the very real differences between children and adults—would be to deny children the full scope of the procedural safeguards that *Miranda* guarantees to adults....

The question remains whether J.D.B. was in custody when police interrogated him. We remand for the state courts to address that question, this time taking account of all of the relevant circumstances of the interrogation, including J.D.B.'s age at the time....

ALITO, J., dissenting.[*]

The Court's decision in this case may seem on first consideration to be modest and sensible, but in truth it is neither. It is fundamentally inconsistent with one of the main justifications for the *Miranda* rule: the perceived need for a clear rule that can be easily applied in all cases. And today's holding is not needed to protect the constitutional rights of minors who are questioned by the police.

---

[*] Chief Justice Roberts and Justices Scalia and Thomas joined this opinion.

Miranda's prophylactic regime places a high value on clarity and certainty…. A key contributor to this clarity, at least up until now, has been *Miranda*'s objective reasonable-person test for determining custody. [In] the interest of simplicity, the custody analysis considers only whether, under the circumstances, a hypothetical reasonable person would consider himself to be confined. Many suspects, of course, will differ from this hypothetical reasonable person….

Today's decision shifts the *Miranda* custody determination from a one-size-fits-all reasonable-person test into an inquiry that must account for at least one individualized characteristic—age—that is thought to correlate with susceptibility to coercive pressures. Age, however, is in no way the only personal characteristic that may correlate with pliability, and in future cases the Court will be forced to choose between two unpalatable alternatives. It may choose to limit today's decision by arbitrarily distinguishing a suspect's age from other personal characteristics—such as intelligence, education, occupation, or prior experience with law enforcement—that may also correlate with susceptibility to coercive pressures. Or, if the Court is unwilling to draw these arbitrary lines, it will be forced to effect a fundamental transformation of the *Miranda* custody test—from a clear, easily applied prophylactic rule into a highly fact-intensive standard resembling the voluntariness test that the *Miranda* Court found to be unsatisfactory. …

I do not dispute that many suspects who are under 18 will be more susceptible to police pressure than the average adult…. It is no less a reality, however, that many persons *over* the age of 18 are also more susceptible to police pressure than the hypothetical reasonable person. Yet the *Miranda* custody standard has never accounted for the personal characteristics of these or any other individual defendants.

Indeed, it has always been the case under *Miranda* that the unusually meek or compliant are subject to the same fixed rules, including the same custody requirement, as those who are unusually resistant to police pressure. *Miranda*'s rigid standards are both overinclusive and underinclusive. They are overinclusive to the extent that they provide a windfall to the most hardened and savvy of suspects, who often have no need for *Miranda*'s protections. And *Miranda*'s requirements are underinclusive to the extent that they fail to account for frailties, idiosyncrasies, and other individualized considerations that might cause a person to bend more easily during a confrontation with the police. Members of this Court have seen this rigidity as a major weakness in

Miranda's "code of rules for confessions." But if it is, then the weakness is an inescapable consequence of the *Miranda* Court's decision to supplement the more holistic voluntariness requirement with a one-size-fits-all prophylactic rule.

That is undoubtedly why this Court's *Miranda* cases have never before mentioned "the suspect's age" or any other individualized consideration in applying the custody standard. And unless the *Miranda* custody rule is now to be radically transformed into one that takes into account the wide range of individual characteristics that are relevant in determining whether a confession is voluntary, the Court must shoulder the burden of explaining why age is different from these other personal characteristics.

Why, for example, is age different from intelligence? Suppose that an officer, upon going to a school to question a student, is told by the principal that the student has an I.Q. of 75 and is in a special-education class. Are those facts more or less important than the student's age in determining whether he or she "felt at liberty to terminate the interrogation and leave"? An I.Q. score, like age, is more than just a number. And an individual's intelligence can also yield conclusions similar to those we have drawn ourselves in cases far afield of *Miranda*.

How about the suspect's cultural background? Suppose the police learn (or should have learned) that a suspect they wish to question is a recent immigrant from a country in which dire consequences often befall any person who dares to attempt to cut short any meeting with the police. Is this really less relevant than the fact that a suspect is a month or so away from his 18th birthday?

The defendant's education is another personal characteristic that may generate "conclusions about behavior and perception." Under today's decision, why should police officers and courts "blind themselves," to the fact that a suspect has "only a fifth-grade education"? Alternatively, what if the police know or should know that the suspect is "a college-educated man with law school training"? How are these individual considerations meaningfully different from age in their relationship to a reasonable person's understanding of his freedom of action? The Court proclaims that a child's age is "different," but the basis for this *ipse dixit* is dubious.

I have little doubt that today's decision will soon be cited by defendants—and perhaps by prosecutors as well—for the proposition that all manner of other individual characteristics should be treated like age and taken into account in the *Miranda* custody calculus. Indeed, there are already lower court decisions that take this approach. [Citing cases from the Ninth Circuit, Arizona, Idaho and Maryland].

Petitioner and the Court attempt to show that [consideration of age in determining custody for purposes of *Miranda*] is not unmanageable by pointing out that ... the age of a defendant is a relevant factor under the reasonable-person standard applicable in negligence suits. But negligence is generally a question for the jury, the members of which can draw on their varied experiences with persons of different ages. It also involves a *post hoc* determination, in the reflective atmosphere of a deliberation room, about whether the defendant conformed to a standard of care. The *Miranda* custody determination, by contrast, must be made in the first instance by police officers in the course of an investigation that may require quick decisionmaking....

Nor do state laws affording extra protection for juveniles during custodial interrogation provide any support for petitioner's arguments. States are free to enact additional restrictions on the police over and above those demanded by the Constitution or *Miranda*. In addition, these state statutes generally create clear, workable rules to guide police conduct. See Brief for Petitioner 16–17 (citing statutes that require or permit parents to be present during custodial interrogation of a minor, that require minors to be advised of a statutory right to communicate with a parent or guardian, and that require parental consent to custodial interrogation). Today's decision, by contrast, injects a new, complicating factor into what had been a clear, easily applied prophylactic rule....

The Court rests its decision to inject personal characteristics into the *Miranda* custody inquiry on the principle that judges applying *Miranda* cannot "blind themselves to ... commonsense reality." But the Court's shift is fundamentally at odds with the clear prophylactic rules that *Miranda* has long enforced. *Miranda* frequently requires judges to blind themselves to the reality that many un-Mirandized custodial confessions are "by no means involuntary" or coerced. It also requires police to provide a rote recitation of *Miranda* warnings that many suspects already know and could likely recite from memory.[13] Under today's new,

---

[13] Surveys have shown that large majorities of the public are aware that "individuals arrested for a crime" have a right to remain silent (81%), a right to a lawyer (95%), and a right to have a lawyer appointed if the arrestee cannot afford one (88%). See Belden, Russonello & Stewart, Developing a National Message for Indigent Defense: Analysis of National Survey 4 (Oct.2001), online at http://www. nlada.org/DMS/Documents/1211996548.53/Pollingresultsreport.pdf.

"reality"-based approach to the doctrine, perhaps these and other principles of our *Miranda* jurisprudence will, like the custody standard, now be ripe for modification. Then, bit by bit, *Miranda* will lose the clarity and ease of application that has long been viewed as one of its chief justifications. I respectfully dissent.

2.   "Triggering" Miranda Warnings

Page 567. Add this material at the end of note 3.

See also Howes v. Fields, 132 S. Ct. 1181 (2012) (rejecting categorical rule that any questioning of a prisoner isolated from the general prison population about an alleged crime based on conduct outside the prison; no "custody" here based on totality of circumstances surrounding interrogation in prison conference room by sheriff's deputies).

Page 575. Add this material to the end of note 4.

See also Joanna Wright, Note, "Mirandizing Terrorists? An Empirical Analysis of the Public Safety Exception, 111 Colum. L. Rev. 1296 (2011).

3.   Form of Warnings

Page 582. Add this material at the end of note 1.

Commonwealth v. McNulty, 937 N.E.2d 16 (Mass. 2010) (state constitution requires police interrogators to inform suspect that he is represented by an attorney who is wanting to advise him, and that the attorney wants the suspect to stop talking to police).

C. *Invocation and Waiver of* Miranda *Rights*

Page 594. Add this material at the end of note 1.

See also Commonwealth v. Clarke, 960 N.E.2d 306 (Mass. 2012) (under state constitution, suspect does not need to invoke right to silence explicitly in order to cut off questioning before waiver of interrogation rights).

E. Sixth Amendment Right to Counsel During Investigations

Page 623. Add this material at the end of note 4.

See also Jewell v. State, 957 N.E.2d 625 (Ind. 2011) (rejecting Texas v. Cobb under state constitution; interrogation without counsel is barred when police ask suspect about uncharged offense that is factually interrelated with another charged offense for which an attorney represents the suspect); People v. Lopez, 947 N.E.2d 1155 (N.Y. 2011) (right to counsel under state constitution bars interrogation of in-custody suspect about any offense if investigators know that suspect has counsel for the offense that is the basis for custody; investigators also must ask suspect about counsel if "there is a probable likelihood" that suspect has counsel for the custodial offense).

Chapter 9

Identifications

B. *Exclusion of Identification Evidence*

2. Exclusion on Due Process Grounds

Page 675. Replace State v. Debose with the following material.

State v. Larry Henderson
27 A.3d 872 (N.J. 2011)

RABNER, C.J.

I. Introduction

In the thirty-four years since the United States Supreme Court announced a test for the admission of eyewitness identification evidence, which New Jersey adopted soon after, a vast body of scientific research about human memory has emerged. That body of work casts doubt on some commonly held views relating to memory. It also calls into question the vitality of the current legal framework for analyzing the reliability of eyewitness identifications. See Manson v. Brathwaite, 432 U.S. 98 (1977); State v. Madison, 536 A.2d 254 (N.J. 1988).

In this case, defendant claims that an eyewitness mistakenly identified him as an accomplice to a murder. Defendant argues that the identification was not reliable because the officers investigating the case intervened during the identification process and unduly influenced the eyewitness. After a pretrial hearing, the trial court found that the officers' behavior was not impermissibly suggestive and admitted the evidence. The Appellate Division reversed. It held that the officers' actions were presumptively suggestive because they violated guidelines issued by the Attorney General in 2001 for conducting identification procedures.

After granting certification and hearing oral argument, we remanded the case and appointed a Special Master to evaluate scientific and other evidence about eyewitness identifications. The Special Master presided over a hearing that probed testimony by seven experts and produced more than 2,000 pages of transcripts along with hundreds of scientific studies. He later issued an extensive and very fine report, much of which we adopt.

We find that the scientific evidence considered at the remand hearing is reliable. That evidence offers convincing proof that the current test for evaluating the trustworthiness of eyewitness identifications should be revised.... It does not offer an adequate measure for reliability or sufficiently deter inappropriate police conduct. It also overstates the jury's inherent ability to evaluate evidence offered by eyewitnesses who honestly believe their testimony is accurate.

Two principal steps are needed to remedy those concerns. First, when defendants can show some evidence of suggestiveness, all relevant system and estimator variables should be explored at pretrial hearings.... Up until now, courts have only considered estimator variables if there was a finding of impermissibly suggestive police conduct.... Second, the court system should develop enhanced jury charges on eyewitness identification for trial judges to use. We anticipate that identification evidence will continue to be admitted in the vast majority of cases. To help jurors weigh that evidence, they must be told about relevant factors and their effect on reliability. To that end, we have asked the Criminal Practice Committee and the Committee on Model Criminal Jury Charges to draft proposed revisions to the current model charge on eyewitness identification and address various system and estimator variables....

The factors that both judges and juries will consider are not etched in stone. We expect that the scientific research underlying them will continue to evolve, as it has in the more than thirty years since *Manson*. For the same reason, police departments are not prevented from improving their practices as we learn more about variables that affect memory. New approaches, though, must be based on reliable scientific evidence that experts generally accept....

II. Facts and Procedural History …

In the early morning hours of January 1, 2003, Rodney Harper was shot to death in an apartment in Camden. James Womble witnessed the murder but did not speak with the police until they approached him ten days later.

Womble and Harper were acquaintances who occasionally socialized at the apartment of Womble's girlfriend, Vivian Williams. On the night of the murder, Womble and Williams brought in the New Year in Williams' apartment by drinking wine and champagne and smoking crack cocaine. Harper had started the evening with them but left at around 10:15 P.M. Williams also left roughly three hours later, leaving Womble alone in the apartment until Harper rejoined him at 2:00 to 2:30 A.M.

Soon after Harper returned, two men forcefully entered the apartment. Womble knew one of them, co-defendant George Clark, who had come to collect $160 from Harper. The other man was a stranger to Womble.

While Harper and Clark went to a different room, the stranger pointed a gun at Womble and told him, "Don't move, stay right here, you're not involved in this." He remained with the stranger in a small, narrow, dark hallway. Womble testified that he "got a look at" the stranger, but not "a real good look." Womble also described the gun pointed at his torso as a dark semiautomatic.

Meanwhile, Womble overheard Clark and Harper argue over money in the other room. At one point, Harper said, "do what you got to do," after which Womble heard a gunshot. Womble then walked into the room, saw Clark holding a handgun, offered to get Clark the $160, and urged him not to shoot Harper again. As Clark left, he warned Womble, "Don't rat me out, I know where you live."

Harper died from the gunshot wound to his chest on January 10, 2003. Camden County Detective Luis Ruiz and Investigator Randall MacNair were assigned to investigate the homicide, and they interviewed Womble the next day. Initially, Womble told the police that he was in the apartment when he heard two gunshots outside, that he left to look for Harper, and that he found Harper slumped over in his car in a nearby parking lot, where Harper said he had been shot by two men he did not know.

The next day, the officers confronted Womble about inconsistencies in his story. Womble claimed that they also threatened to charge him in connection with the murder. Womble then decided to "come clean." He admitted that he lied at first because he did not want to "rat" out anyone and "didn't want to get involved" out of fear of retaliation against his elderly father. Womble led the investigators to Clark, who eventually gave a statement about his involvement and identified the person who accompanied him as defendant Larry Henderson.

The officers had Womble view a photographic array on January 14, 2003. That event lies at the heart of this decision and is discussed in greater detail below. Ultimately, Womble identified defendant from the array, and Investigator MacNair prepared a warrant for his arrest. Upon arrest, defendant admitted to the police that he had accompanied Clark to the apartment where Harper was killed, and heard a gunshot while waiting in the hallway. But defendant denied witnessing or participating in the shooting....

The trial court conducted a pretrial *Wade* hearing to determine the admissibility of [Womble's] identification. United States v. Wade, 388 U.S. 218 (1967). Investigator MacNair, Detective Ruiz, and Womble all testified at the hearing. Cherry Hill Detective Thomas Weber also testified.

Detective Weber conducted the identification procedure because, consistent with guidelines issued by the Attorney General, he was not a primary investigator in the case. According to the Guidelines ... primary investigators should not administer photo or live lineup identification procedures "to ensure that inadvertent verbal cues or body language do not impact on a witness."

Ruiz and MacNair gave Weber an array consisting of seven "filler" photos and one photo of defendant Henderson. The eight photos all depicted headshots of African–American men between the ages of twenty-eight and thirty-five, with short hair, goatees, and, according to Weber, similar facial features. At the hearing, Weber was not asked whether he knew which photograph depicted the suspect. (Later at trial, he said he did not know.)

The identification procedure took place in an interview room in the Prosecutor's Office. At first, Weber and Womble were alone in the room. Weber began by reading [cautionary] instructions off a standard form....

Detective Weber pre-numbered the eight photos, shuffled them, and showed them to Womble one at a time. Womble quickly eliminated five of the photos. He then reviewed the remaining three, discounted one more, and said he "wasn't 100 percent sure of the final two pictures." At the *Wade* hearing, Detective Weber recalled that Womble "just shook his head a lot. He seemed indecisive." But he did not express any fear to Weber.

Weber left the room with the photos and informed MacNair and Ruiz that the witness had narrowed the pictures to two but could not make a final identification. MacNair and Ruiz testified at the hearing that they did not know whether defendant's picture was among the remaining two photos.

MacNair and Ruiz entered the interview room to speak with Womble. According to MacNair's testimony at the *Wade* hearing, he and Ruiz believed that Womble was holding back—as he had earlier in the investigation—based on fear. Ruiz said Womble was "nervous, upset about his father."

In an effort to calm Womble, MacNair testified that he "just told him to focus, to calm down, to relax and that any type of protection that [he] would need, any threats against [him] would be put to rest by the Police Department." Ruiz added, "just do what you have to do, and we'll be out of here." In response, according to MacNair, Womble said he "could make [an] identification."

MacNair and Ruiz then left the interview room. Ruiz testified that the entire exchange lasted less than one minute; Weber believed it took about five minutes. When Weber returned to the room, he reshuffled the eight photos and again displayed them to Womble sequentially. This time, when Womble saw defendant's photo, he slammed his hand on the table and exclaimed, "that's the mother [- - - - - -] there." From start to finish, the entire process took fifteen minutes.

Womble did not recant his identification, but during the *Wade* hearing he testified that he felt as though Detective Weber was "nudging" him to choose defendant's photo, and "that there was pressure" to make a choice.

After hearing the testimony, the trial court ... found that the photo display itself was "a fair makeup." Under the totality of the circumstances, the judge concluded that the photo identification was reliable. The court found that there was "nothing in this case that was improper, and certainly nothing that was so suggestive as to result in a substantial likelihood of misidentification at all." The court also noted that Womble displayed no doubts about identifying defendant Henderson, that he had the opportunity to view defendant at the crime scene, and that Womble fixed his attention on defendant "because he had a gun on him." ...

The following facts—relevant to Womble's identification of defendant—were adduced at trial after the court determined that the identification was admissible: Womble smoked two bags of crack cocaine with his girlfriend in the hours before the shooting; the two also consumed one bottle of champagne and one bottle of wine; the lighting was "pretty dark" in the hallway where Womble and defendant interacted; defendant shoved Womble during the incident; and Womble remembered looking at the gun pointed at his chest. Womble also admitted smoking about two bags of crack cocaine each day from the time of the shooting until speaking with police ten days later.

At trial, Womble elaborated on his state of mind during the identification procedure. He testified that when he first looked at the photo array, he did not see anyone he recognized. As he explained, "my mind was drawing a blank ... so I just started eliminating photos." To make a final identification, Womble said that he "really had to search deep." He was nonetheless "sure" of the identification....

Neither Clark nor defendant testified at trial. The primary evidence against defendant, thus, was Womble's identification and Detective MacNair's testimony about defendant's post-arrest statement.

At the close of trial on July 20, 2004, the court relied on the existing model jury charge on eyewitness identification. [Later that day], the jury acquitted defendant of murder and aggravated manslaughter, and convicted him of reckless manslaughter, aggravated assault, and two weapons charges.... The court sentenced him to an aggregate eleven-year term of imprisonment, with a period of parole ineligibility of almost six years....

The Appellate Division presumed that the identification procedure in this case was impermissibly suggestive under the first prong of the *Manson/Madison* test. The court reversed and remanded for a new *Wade* hearing to determine whether the identification was nonetheless reliable under the test's second prong. The panel anchored its finding to what it considered to be a material breach of the Attorney General Guidelines....

We granted the State's petition for certification, and also granted leave to appear as amicus curiae to the Association of Criminal Defense Lawyers of New Jersey (ACDL) and the Innocence Project (collectively "amici"). In their briefs and at oral argument, the parties and amici raised questions about possible shortcomings in the *Manson/Madison* test in light of recent scientific research. In an unpublished Order ... we concluded that an inadequate factual record existed on which to test the current validity of our state law standards on the admissibility of eyewitness identification. We therefore remanded the matter [and] appointed the Honorable Geoffrey Gaulkin, P.J.A.D. (retired and temporarily assigned on recall) to preside at the remand hearing as a Special Master. The parties and amici collectively produced more than 360 exhibits, which included more than 200 published scientific studies on human memory and eyewitness identification. During the ten-day remand hearing, the Special Master heard testimony from seven expert witnesses. ...

III. Proof of Misidentifications

[Misidentification] is widely recognized as the single greatest cause of wrongful convictions in this country.... Nationwide, more than seventy-five percent of convictions overturned due to DNA evidence involved eyewitness misidentification. In half of the cases, eyewitness testimony was not corroborated by confessions, forensic science, or informants. Thirty-six percent of the defendants convicted were misidentified by more than one eyewitness....

New Jersey is not immune. The parties noted that misidentifications factored into three of the five reported DNA exonerations in our State. In one of those cases, this Court had reversed convictions for rape and robbery because the trial court failed to instruct the jury that people may have greater difficulty in identifying members of a different race. See State v. Cromedy, 727 A.2d 457 (N.J. 1999). After the decision, DNA tests led to Cromedy's exoneration.

But DNA exonerations are rare. To determine whether statistics from such cases reflect system-wide flaws, police departments have allowed social scientists to analyze case files and observe and record data from real-world identification procedures. [The Court reviewed a variety of published studies aiming to determine how often innocent suspects are wrongly identified, and concluded that any] one of the above studies, standing alone, reveals a troubling lack of reliability in eyewitness identifications.

[A] concept called relative judgment, which the Special Master and the experts discussed, helps explain how people make identifications and raises concerns about reliability. Under typical lineup conditions, eyewitnesses are asked to identify a suspect from a group of similar-looking people. "Relative judgment refers to the fact that the witness seems to be choosing the lineup member who most resembles the witnesses' memory *relative* to other lineup members." Gary L. Wells, The Psychology of Lineup Identifications, 14 J. Applied Soc. Psychol. 89, 92 (1984) (emphasis in original). As a result, if the actual perpetrator is not in a lineup, people may be inclined to choose the best look-alike....

We presume that jurors are able to detect liars from truth tellers. But as scholars have cautioned, most eyewitnesses think they are telling the truth even when their testimony is inaccurate, and because the eyewitness is testifying honestly (i.e., sincerely), he or she will not display the demeanor of the dishonest or biased witness. Instead, some mistaken eyewitnesses, at least by the time they testify at trial, exude supreme confidence in their identifications....

IV. Current Legal Framework

The current standards for determining the admissibility of eyewitness identification evidence derive from the principles the United States Supreme Court set forth in Manson v. Brathwaite, 432 U.S. 98 (1977); State v. Madison, 536 A.2d 254 (N.J. 1988).... *Madison* succinctly outlined *Manson*'s two-step test as follows:

> [A] court must first decide whether the procedure in question was in fact impermissibly suggestive. If the court does find the procedure impermissibly suggestive, it must then decide whether the objectionable procedure resulted in a "very substantial likelihood of irreparable misidentification." In carrying out the second part of the analysis, the court will focus on the reliability of the identification. If the court finds that the identification is reliable despite the impermissibly suggestive nature of the procedure, the identification may be admitted into evidence....

To assess reliability, courts must consider five factors adopted from Neil v. Biggers, 409 U.S. 188 (1972): (1) the "opportunity of the witness to view the criminal at the time of the crime"; (2) "the witness's degree of attention"; (3) "the accuracy of his prior description of the criminal"; (4) "the level of certainty demonstrated at the time of the confrontation"; and (5) "the time between the crime and the confrontation." Those factors are to be weighed against the corrupting effect of the suggestive identification itself.

Procedurally, a defendant must first proffer some evidence of impermissible suggestiveness to be entitled to a *Wade* hearing. At the hearing, if the court decides the procedure "was in fact impermissibly suggestive," it then considers the reliability factors. The State then has the burden of proving by clear and convincing evidence that the identification had a source independent of the police-conducted identification procedures. Overall, the reliability determination is to be made from the totality of the circumstances....

Since *Madison,* this Court, on occasion, has refined the *Manson/ Madison* framework. [In] State v. Romero, 922 A.2d 693 (N.J. 2007), the Court recognized that jurors likely will believe eyewitness testimony "when it is offered with a high level of confidence," even though the accuracy of an eyewitness and the confidence of that witness may not be related to one another at all. The Court [directed trial judges to instruct juries about the particular risks of such eyewitness testimony]. In State v. Delgado, 902 A.2d 888 (N.J. 2006), the Court directed that law enforcement officers make a written record detailing all out-of-court identification procedures, including the place where the procedure was conducted, the dialogue between the witness and the interlocutor, and the results.

Despite those important, incremental changes, we have repeatedly used the *Manson/Madison* test to determine the admissibility of eyewitness identification evidence. [A proper record convinces us now that a different approach is required. The record] enables us to consider whether the *Manson/Madison* framework remains valid and appropriate or if a different approach is required. To make that determination, we first look to the scope of the scientific evidence since 1977. We then examine its content.

V. Scope of Scientific Research

... During the 1970s, when the Supreme Court decided *Manson,* researchers conducted some experiments on the malleability of human memory. But according to expert testimony, that decade produced only four published articles in psychology literature containing the words "eyewitness" and "identity" in their abstracts. By contrast, the Special Master estimated that more than two thousand studies related to eyewitness identification have been published in the past thirty years.

Some recent studies have successfully gathered real-world data from actual police identification procedures. But most eyewitness identification research is conducted through controlled lab experiments.... Although one lab experiment can produce intriguing results, its data set may be small. For example, if only twenty people participated in an experiment, it may be difficult to generalize the results beyond the individual study. Meta-analysis aims to solve that problem. A meta-analysis is a synthesis of all obtainable data collected in a specified topical area.... More than twenty-five meta-analyses were presented at the hearing. [Identification] statistics from across the studies were remarkably consistent: [the studies of all types consistently found that something approaching] 24% of witnesses identified fillers. Those statistics are similar to data from real cases. [In] police investigations in Sacramento and London [examined later by researchers], roughly 20% of eyewitnesses identified fillers. Thus, although lab and field experiments may be imperfect proxies for real-world conditions, certain data they have produced are relevant and persuasive....

VI. How Memory Works

[Eyewitness identification research] reveals that an array of variables can affect and dilute memory and lead to misidentifications. Scientific literature divides those variables into two categories: system and estimator variables. System variables are factors like lineup procedures which are within the control of the criminal justice system. Estimator variables are factors related to the witness, the perpetrator, or the event itself—like distance, lighting, or stress—over which the legal system has no control.

[The Court reviewed the scientific evidence in the Special Master's report and concluded that several system variables increase the likelihood of misidentification. These include a failure to perform blind lineup procedures; a failure to give proper pre-lineup instructions to the witness; a lineup that does not place the suspect in an array of look-alikes; a lineup with less than five fillers, or featuring more than one suspect; providing confirmatory feedback to the witness after he or she identifies the suspect; giving a witness more than one viewing of the same suspect in different identification efforts; and use of showups conducted more than two hours after an event. The Court also required law enforcement officers to make a full record of the witness' statement of confidence after making an identification. The Court decided that the scientific evidence was inconclusive on the question of whether a lineup should be constructed to match the witness' initial description of the perpetrator or to match the appearance of the suspect; whether investigators should use simultaneous or sequential lineups; and whether they should use artists' composite drawings of a suspect.

The Court also reviewed the scientific evidence regarding estimator variables, and concluded that several variables are likely to affect the reliability of an identification. These include high levels of stress for the witness during the event; the presence of a visible weapon during a brief interaction; brief or fleeting time available to observe an event; reliance on a witness who is intoxicated, or a witness who is a child; a large age gap between the witness and the observed party; the use of a disguise by the perpetrator; a large time gap between the event and the identification; cross-racial identifications; and feedback from co-witnesses. The Court ordered law enforcement offices to ask witnesses, as part of the identification process, questions designed to elicit whether the witness spoke with anyone about the identification; the Court also ordered the police to record the witness' answers.]

Some of the findings described above are intuitive. Everyone knows, for instance, that bad lighting conditions make it more difficult to perceive the details of a person's face. Some findings are less obvious. Although many may believe that witnesses to a highly stressful, threatening event will "never forget a face" because of their intense focus at the time, the research suggests that is not necessarily so.

Using survey questionnaires and mock-jury studies, experts have attempted to discern what lay people understand, and what information about perception and memory are beyond the ken of the average juror. Based on those studies, the Special Master found "that laypersons are largely unfamiliar" with scientific findings and "often hold beliefs to the contrary." ...

Neither juror surveys nor mock-jury studies can offer definitive proof of what jurors know or believe about memory. But they reveal generally that people do not intuitively understand all of the relevant scientific findings. As a result, there is a need to promote greater juror understanding of those issues....

VII. Responses to Scientific Studies

Beyond the scientific community, law enforcement and reform agencies across the nation have taken note of the scientific findings. In turn, they have formed task forces and recommended or implemented new procedures to improve the reliability of eyewitness identifications.

New Jersey has been at the forefront of that effort. In 2001, under the leadership of then-Attorney General John J. Farmer, Jr., New Jersey became the first state in the Nation to officially adopt the recommendations issued by the Department of Justice and issue guidelines for preparing and conducting identification procedures.... The Attorney General Guidelines are thorough and exacting. We once again commend the Attorney General's Office for responding to important social scientific evidence and promoting the reliability of eyewitness identifications. Since 2001, when the recommended Guidelines went into effect, they may well have prevented wrongful convictions.

However, the Guidelines are a series of recommended best practices. The Attorney General expressly noted that identifications that do not follow the recommended Guidelines should not be deemed "inadmissible or otherwise in error." Although the State argues that the Court should defer to other branches of government to deal with the evolving social scientific landscape, it remains the Court's obligation to guarantee that constitutional requirements are met, and to ensure the integrity of criminal trials.

Other state and local authorities have instituted similar changes to their eyewitness identification procedures. In 2005, for example, the Attorney General of Wisconsin issued a set of identification guidelines recommending, among other things, "double-blind, sequential photo arrays and lineups with non-suspect fillers chosen to minimize suggestiveness, non-biased instructions to eyewitnesses, and assessments of confidence immediately after identifications." Office of the Attorney Gen., Wis. Dep't of Justice, Model Policy and Procedure for Eyewitness Identification 1 (2005); see also Dallas Police Dep't, Dallas Police Department General Order § 304.01 (2009); Denver Police Dep't, Operations Manual § 104.44 (2006); Police Chiefs' Ass'n of Santa Clara County, Line-up Protocol for Law Enforcement (2002). North Carolina was among the first states to pass legislation mandating, among other things, pre-lineup instructions and blind and sequential lineup administration. Illinois, Maryland, Ohio, West Virginia, and Wisconsin have passed similar laws regarding lineup practices.

VIII. Parties' Arguments

... The State argues vigorously against the Appellate Division's holding that a breach of the Attorney General Guidelines results in a presumption of impermissible suggestiveness. The State contends that such an approach would penalize the Attorney General for adopting Guidelines designed to improve identification practices, and reward defendants who intimidate witnesses....

Because eyewitness identification science is probabilistic—meaning that it cannot determine if a particular identification is accurate—the State also argues that the legal system should continue to rely on jurors to assess the credibility of eyewitnesses. To guide juries, the State favors appropriate, flexible jury instructions. The State maintains that expert testimony is not advisable because the relevant subjects are not beyond the ken of the average juror....

Defendant embraces the decision of the Appellate Division and agrees that a violation of the Attorney General Guidelines should create a presumption of impermissible suggestiveness. With regard to the *Manson/Madison* test, defendant and amici argue that more than thirty years of scientific evidence undercut the assumptions underlying the Supreme Court's decision in *Manson*. They [point out that] courts only consider the five reliability factors in *Manson/Madison* after finding suggestiveness, even though some of those factors may themselves be unreliable because of suggestive police behavior; [the] all-or-nothing remedy of suppression is too inflexible; ... and it does not deter suggestive police procedures.

To correct those flaws, defendant and the ACDL initially proposed two alternative frameworks to replace *Manson/Madison*. Among other arguments, they analogized to Miranda v. Arizona, 384 U.S. 436 (1966), and argued that eyewitness evidence should be excluded per se if an identification procedure violated the Attorney General Guidelines or if a judge found other evidence of suggestiveness.

Consistent with the Special Master's report, they now urge this Court to require a reliability hearing in every case in which the State intends to present identification evidence. At the hearing, they submit that a wide range of system and estimator variables would be relevant, and the State should bear the burden of establishing reliability....

IX. Legal Conclusions ...

To protect due process concerns, the *Manson* Court's two-part test rested on three assumptions: (1) that it would adequately measure the reliability of eyewitness testimony; (2) that the test's focus on suggestive police procedure would deter improper practices; and (3) that jurors would recognize and discount untrustworthy eyewitness testimony. We remanded this case to determine whether those assumptions and other factors reflected in the two-part *Manson/Madison* test are still valid. We conclude from the hearing that they are not....

First, under *Manson/Madison*, defendants must show that police procedures were "impermissibly suggestive" before courts can consider estimator variables that also bear on reliability. As a result, although evidence of relevant estimator variables tied to the Neil v. Biggers factors is routinely introduced at pretrial hearings, their effect is ignored unless there is a finding of impermissibly suggestive police conduct. In this case, for example, the testimony at the *Wade* hearing related principally to the lineup procedure. Because the court found that the procedure was not "impermissibly suggestive," details about the witness' use of drugs and alcohol, the dark lighting conditions, the presence of a weapon pointed at the witness' chest, and other estimator variables that affect reliability were not considered at the hearing. (They were explored later at trial.)

Second, under *Manson/Madison*, if a court finds that the police used impermissibly suggestive identification procedures, the trial judge then weighs the corrupting effect of the process against five "reliability" factors. But three of those factors—the opportunity to view the crime, the witness' degree of attention, and the level of certainty at the time of the identification—rely on self-reporting by eyewitnesses; and research has shown that those reports can be skewed by the suggestive procedures themselves and thus may not be reliable....

Third, rather than act as a deterrent, the *Manson/Madison* test may unintentionally reward suggestive police practices. The irony of the current test is that the more suggestive the procedure, the greater the chance eyewitnesses will seem confident and report better viewing conditions. Courts in turn are encouraged to admit identifications based on criteria that have been tainted by the very suggestive practices the test aims to deter.

Fourth, the *Manson/Madison* test addresses only one option for questionable eyewitness identification evidence: suppression. Yet few judges choose that ultimate sanction. An all-or-nothing approach does not account for the complexities of eyewitness identification evidence....

Remedying the problems with the current *Manson/Madison* test requires an approach that addresses its shortcomings: one that allows judges to consider all relevant factors that affect reliability in deciding whether an identification is admissible; that is not heavily weighted by factors that can be corrupted by suggestiveness; that promotes deterrence in a meaningful way; and that focuses on helping jurors both understand

and evaluate the effects that various factors have on memory—because we recognize that most identifications will be admitted in evidence. [The] revised framework should allow all relevant system *and* estimator variables to be explored and weighed at pretrial hearings when there is some actual evidence of suggestiveness; and second, courts should develop and use enhanced jury charges to help jurors evaluate eyewitness identification evidence....

With that in mind, we first outline the revised approach for evaluating identification evidence and then explain its details and the reasoning behind it. First, to obtain a pretrial hearing, a defendant has the initial burden of showing some evidence of suggestiveness that could lead to a mistaken identification. That evidence, in general, must be tied to a system—and not an estimator—variable.

Second, the State must then offer proof to show that the proffered eyewitness identification is reliable—accounting for system and estimator variables—subject to the following: the court can end the hearing at any time if it finds from the testimony that defendant's threshold allegation of suggestiveness is groundless....

Third, the ultimate burden remains on the defendant to prove a very substantial likelihood of irreparable misidentification. To do so, a defendant can cross-examine eyewitnesses and police officials and present witnesses and other relevant evidence linked to system and estimator variables.

Fourth, if after weighing the evidence presented a court finds from the totality of the circumstances that defendant has demonstrated a very substantial likelihood of irreparable misidentification, the court should suppress the identification evidence. If the evidence is admitted, the court should provide appropriate, tailored jury instructions....

To evaluate whether there is evidence of suggestiveness to trigger a hearing, courts should consider the following non-exhaustive list of system variables:

1. *Blind Administration.* Was the lineup procedure performed double-blind? If double-blind testing was impractical, did the police use a technique ... to ensure that the administrator had no knowledge of where the suspect appeared in the photo array or lineup?

2. *Pre-identification Instructions.* Did the administrator provide neutral, pre-identification instructions warning that the suspect may not be present in the lineup and that the witness should not feel compelled to make an identification?

3. *Lineup Construction.* Did the array or lineup contain only one suspect embedded among at least five innocent fillers? Did the suspect stand out from other members of the lineup?

4. *Feedback.* Did the witness receive any information or feedback, about the suspect or the crime, before, during, or after the identification procedure?

5. *Recording Confidence.* Did the administrator record the witness' statement of confidence immediately after the identification, before the possibility of any confirmatory feedback?

6. *Multiple Viewings.* Did the witness view the suspect more than once as part of multiple identification procedures? Did police use the same fillers more than once?

7. *Showups.* Did the police perform a showup more than two hours after an event? Did the police warn the witness that the suspect may not be the perpetrator and that the witness should not feel compelled to make an identification?

8. *Private Actors.* Did law enforcement elicit from the eyewitness whether he or she had spoken with anyone about the identification and, if so, what was discussed?

9. *Other Identifications Made.* Did the eyewitness initially make no choice or choose a different suspect or filler?

The court should conduct a *Wade* hearing only if defendant offers some evidence of suggestiveness. If, however, at any time during the hearing the trial court concludes from the testimony that defendant's initial claim of suggestiveness is baseless, and if no other evidence of suggestiveness has been demonstrated by the evidence, the court may exercise its discretion to end the hearing. Under those circumstances, the court need not permit the defendant or require the State to elicit more evidence about estimator variables; that evidence would be reserved for the jury....

If some actual proof of suggestiveness remains, courts should consider the above system variables as well as the following non-exhaustive list of estimator variables to evaluate the overall reliability of an identification and determine its admissibility:

1. *Stress.* Did the event involve a high level of stress?

2. *Weapon focus.* Was a visible weapon used during a crime of short duration?

3. *Duration.* How much time did the witness have to observe the event?

4. *Distance and Lighting.* How close were the witness and perpetrator? What were the lighting conditions at the time?

5. *Witness Characteristics.* Was the witness under the influence of alcohol or drugs? Was age a relevant factor under the circumstances of the case?

6. *Characteristics of Perpetrator.* Was the culprit wearing a disguise? Did the suspect have different facial features at the time of the identification?

7. *Memory decay.* How much time elapsed between the crime and the identification?

8. *Race-bias.* Does the case involve a cross-racial identification? ...

The above factors are not exclusive. Nor are they intended to be frozen in time. We recognize that scientific research relating to the reliability of eyewitness evidence is dynamic; the field is very different today than it was in 1977, and it will likely be quite different thirty years from now. By providing the above lists, we do not intend to hamstring police departments or limit them from improving practices. Likewise, we do not limit trial courts from reviewing evolving, substantial, and generally accepted scientific research. But to the extent the police undertake new practices, or courts either consider variables differently or entertain new ones, they must rely on reliable scientific evidence that is generally accepted by experts in the community.

We adopt this approach over the initial recommendation of defendant and the ACDL that any violation of the Attorney General Guidelines should require per se exclusion of the resulting eyewitness identification. Although that approach might yield greater deterrence, it could also lead to the loss of a substantial amount of reliable evidence. We believe that the more flexible framework outlined above protects defendants' right to a fair trial at the same time it enables the State to meet its responsibility to ensure public safety.

[Concerns] about estimator variables alone cannot trigger a pretrial hearing; only system variables would.... Several reasons favor the approach we outline today. First, we anticipate that eyewitness identification evidence will likely not be ruled inadmissible at pretrial hearings solely on account of estimator variables. For example, it is difficult to imagine that a trial judge would preclude a witness from testifying because the lighting was "too dark," the witness was "too distracted" by the presence of a weapon, or he or she was under "too much" stress while making an observation. How dark is too dark as a matter of law? How much is too much? What guideposts would a trial judge use in making those judgment calls? In all likelihood, the witness would be allowed to testify before a jury and face cross-examination designed to probe the weaknesses of her identification. Jurors would also have the benefit of enhanced instructions to evaluate that testimony— even when there is no evidence of suggestiveness in the case. As a result, a pretrial hearing triggered by, and focused on, estimator variables would likely not screen out identification evidence and would largely be duplicated at trial.

Second, courts cannot affect estimator variables; by definition, they relate to matters outside the control of law enforcement. More probing pretrial hearings about suggestive police procedures, though, can deter inappropriate police practices.

Third, as demonstrated above, suggestive behavior can distort various other factors that are weighed in assessing reliability. That warrants a greater pretrial focus on system variables.

Fourth, we are mindful of the practical impact of today's ruling. Because defendants will now be free to explore a broader range of estimator variables at pretrial hearings to assess the reliability of an identification, those hearings will become more intricate. They will routinely involve testimony from both the police and eyewitnesses, and that testimony will likely expand as more substantive areas are explored. Also, trial courts will retain discretion to allow expert testimony at pretrial hearings.

In 2009, trial courts in New Jersey conducted roughly 200 *Wade* hearings, according to the Administrative Office of the Courts. If estimator variables alone could trigger a hearing, that number might increase to nearly all cases in which eyewitness identification evidence plays a part. We have to measure that outcome in light of the following reality that the Special Master observed: judges rarely suppress eyewitness evidence at pretrial hearings. Therefore, to allow hearings in the majority of identification cases might overwhelm the system with little resulting benefit....

As is true today, juries will continue to hear about all relevant system and estimator variables at trial, through direct and cross-examination and arguments by counsel. In addition, when identification is at issue in a case, trial courts will continue to provide appropriate guidelines to focus the jury's attention on how to analyze and consider the trustworthiness of eyewitness identification. Based on the record developed on remand, we direct that enhanced instructions be given to guide juries about the various factors that may affect the reliability of an identification in a particular case....

Expert testimony may also be introduced at trial, but only if otherwise appropriate. The Rules of Evidence permit expert testimony to "assist the trier of fact to understand the evidence or to determine a fact in issue." N.J.R.E. 702. ... Finally, in rare cases, judges may use their discretion to redact parts of identification testimony.... For example, if an eyewitness' confidence was not properly recorded soon after an identification procedure, and evidence revealed that the witness received confirmatory feedback from the police or a co-witness, the court can bar potentially distorted and unduly prejudicial statements about the witness' level of confidence from being introduced at trial....

To help implement this decision, we ask the Criminal Practice Committee and the Committee on Model Criminal Jury Charges to draft proposed revisions to the current charge on eyewitness identification and submit them to this Court for review before they are implemented. Specifically, we ask them to consider all of the system and estimator variables in section VI for which we have found scientific support that is generally accepted by experts, and to modify the current model charge accordingly....

XI. Application

We return to the facts of this case. After Womble, the eyewitness, informed the lineup administrator that he could not make an identification from the final two photos, the investigating officers intervened. They told Womble to focus and calm down, and assured him that the police would protect him from retaliation. "Just do what you have to do," they instructed. From that exchange, Womble could reasonably infer that there was an identification to be made, and that he would be protected if he made it. The officers conveyed that basic message to him as they encouraged him to make an identification.

The suggestive nature of the officers' comments entitled defendant to a pretrial hearing, and he received one. Applying the *Manson/ Madison* test, the trial judge admitted the evidence. We now remand to the trial court for an expanded hearing consistent with the principles outlined in this decision. Defendant may probe all relevant system and estimator variables at the hearing. In addition to suggestiveness, the trial court should consider Womble's drug and alcohol use immediately before the confrontation, weapon focus, and lighting, among other relevant factors. We express no view on the outcome of the hearing....

For the reasons set forth above, we modify and affirm the judgment of the Appellate Division, and modify the framework for assessing eyewitness identification evidence in criminal cases. We remand to the trial court for further proceedings consistent with this opinion.

Page 687.   Add this material at the end of note 2.

The Supreme Court in Perry v. New Hampshire, 132 S. Ct. 716 (2012), declined an invitation to update the legal framework that governs due process claims in this area. The Court held that due process does not require a trial judge to determine the reliability of eyewitness testimony unless a defendant establishes as a preliminary matter that the identification procedure was "unduly suggestive." The exclusion of evidence before trial is designed to prevent police misconduct, but not necessarily to prevent the use of inaccurate evidence; the ultimate reliability of the evidence used to convict a defendant is entrusted instead to juries at trial.

C. Other Remedies for Improper Identification Procedures

Page 700.   Add this material at the end of note 6.

See also Heather D. Flowe, Amrita Mehta & Ebbe B. Ebbesen, The Role of Eyewitness Identification Evidence in Felony Case Dispositions, 17 Psychol. Pub. Pol'y & L. 140 (2011) (examining role of eyewitness identification evidence in felony issuing decisions in one large District Attorney's office).

Chapter 11

Defense Counsel

A. When Will Counsel Be Provided?

2. Types of Proceedings

Page 781.   Add this material at the end of note 1.

The Supreme Court in Turner v. Rogers, 131 S. Ct. 2507 (2011), considered the right to appointed counsel during civil proceedings that can lead to imprisonment for a spouse who fails to make court-ordered child support payments and as a result is held in contempt of court. Michael Turner failed to make numerous child support payments. A judge in the Family Court ultimately found him in contempt of court and ordered him to serve a twelve-month jail term. The Supreme Court concluded that appointed counsel is not strictly necessary for the respondent in such civil proceedings, so long as the complaining party is also unrepresented by counsel, the respondent receives notice that his ability to pay the arrears will be the critical issue, and the court creates adequate opportunities to learn about his ability to pay. Because Turner received neither appointed counsel nor such "alternative procedural safeguards" in the civil contempt proceedings in this case, the Court ruled that his imprisonment violated due process.

C. Adequacy of Counsel

Page 807.   Add this material before the notes.

Blaine Lafler v. Anthony Cooper
132 S. Ct. 1376 (2012)

KENNEDY, J.[*]

In this case ... a criminal defendant seeks a remedy when inadequate assistance of counsel caused non-acceptance of a plea offer and further proceedings led to a less favorable outcome. [A] favorable plea offer was reported to the client but, on advice of counsel, was rejected. [After] the plea offer had been rejected, there was a full and fair trial before a jury. After a guilty verdict, the defendant received a sentence harsher than that offered in the rejected plea bargain. The instant case comes to the Court with the concession that counsel's advice with respect to the plea offer fell below the standard of adequate assistance of counsel guaranteed by the Sixth Amendment....

I

On the evening of March 25, 2003, respondent pointed a gun toward Kali Mundy's head and fired. From the record, it is unclear why respondent did this, and at trial it was suggested that he might have acted either in self-defense or in defense of another person. In any event the shot missed and Mundy fled. Respondent followed in pursuit, firing repeatedly. Mundy was shot in her buttock, hip, and abdomen but survived the assault.

Respondent was charged under Michigan law with assault with intent to murder, possession of a firearm by a felon, possession of a firearm in the commission of a felony, misdemeanor possession of marijuana, and for being a habitual offender. On two occasions, the prosecution offered to dismiss two of the charges and to recommend a sentence of 51 to 85 months for the other two, in exchange for a guilty plea. In a communication with the court respondent admitted guilt and expressed a willingness to accept the offer. Respondent, however, later rejected the offer on both occasions, allegedly after his attorney convinced him that the prosecution would be unable to establish his intent to murder Mundy

---

[*] Justices Ginsburg, Breyer, Sotomayor, and Kagan joined this opinion.

because she had been shot below the waist. On the first day of trial the prosecution offered a significantly less favorable plea deal, which respondent again rejected. After trial, respondent was convicted on all counts and received a mandatory minimum sentence of 185 to 360 months' imprisonment.

In a so-called *Ginther* hearing before the state trial court, see People v. Ginther, 212 N.W.2d 922 (Mich. 1973), respondent argued his attorney's advice to reject the plea constituted ineffective assistance. The trial judge rejected the claim [and the appellate courts in Michigan followed suit]. Respondent then filed a petition for federal habeas relief under 28 U.S.C. § 2254, renewing his ineffective-assistance-of-counsel claim. After finding, as required by the Antiterrorism and Effective Death Penalty Act of 1996 (AEDPA), that the Michigan Court of Appeals had unreasonably applied the constitutional standards for effective assistance of counsel laid out in Strickland v. Washington, 466 U.S. 668 (1984), and Hill v. Lockhart, 474 U.S. 52 (1985), the District Court granted a conditional writ. To remedy the violation, the District Court ordered specific performance of respondent's original plea agreement, for a minimum sentence in the range of fifty-one to eighty-five months. The United States Court of Appeals for the Sixth Circuit affirmed....

II A

Defendants have a Sixth Amendment right to counsel, a right that extends to the plea-bargaining process. During plea negotiations defendants are entitled to the effective assistance of competent counsel. In Hill v. Lockhart, 474 U.S. 52 (1985), the Court held "the two-part Strickland v. Washington test applies to challenges to guilty pleas based on ineffective assistance of counsel." The performance prong of *Strickland* requires a defendant to show "that counsel's representation fell below an objective standard of reasonableness." In this case all parties agree the performance of respondent's counsel was deficient when he advised respondent to reject the plea offer on the grounds he could not be convicted at trial. In light of this concession, it is unnecessary for this Court to explore the issue.

The question for this Court is how to apply *Strickland*'s prejudice test where ineffective assistance results in a rejection of the plea offer and the defendant is convicted at the ensuing trial.

B

To establish *Strickland* prejudice a defendant must "show that there is a reasonable probability that, but for counsel's unprofessional errors, the result of the proceeding would have been different." In the context of pleas a defendant must show the outcome of the plea process would have been different with competent advice. In *Hill*, when evaluating the petitioner's claim that ineffective assistance led to the improvident acceptance of a guilty plea, the Court required the petitioner to show "that there is a reasonable probability that, but for counsel's errors, [the defendant] would not have pleaded guilty and would have insisted on going to trial."

In contrast to *Hill*, here the ineffective advice led not to an offer's acceptance but to its rejection. Having to stand trial, not choosing to waive it, is the prejudice alleged. In these circumstances a defendant must show that but for the ineffective advice of counsel there is a reasonable probability that the plea offer would have been presented to the court (*i.e.,* that the defendant would have accepted the plea and the prosecution would not have withdrawn it in light of intervening circumstances), that the court would have accepted its terms, and that the conviction or sentence, or both, under the offer's terms would have been less severe than under the judgment and sentence that in fact were imposed....

Petitioner and the Solicitor General propose a different, far more narrow, view of the Sixth Amendment. They contend there can be no finding of *Strickland* prejudice arising from plea bargaining if the defendant is later convicted at a fair trial. The three reasons petitioner and the Solicitor General offer for their approach are unpersuasive.

First, petitioner and the Solicitor General claim that the sole purpose of the Sixth Amendment is to protect the right to a fair trial. Errors before trial, they argue, are not cognizable under the Sixth Amendment unless they affect the fairness of the trial itself. The Sixth Amendment, however, is not so narrow in its reach. The Sixth Amendment requires effective assistance of counsel at critical stages of a criminal proceeding. Its protections are not designed simply to protect the trial, even though "counsel's absence [in these stages] may derogate from the accused's right to a fair trial." United States v. Wade, 388 U.S. 218, 226 (1967). The constitutional guarantee applies to pretrial critical stages that are part of the whole course of a criminal proceeding, a proceeding in which defendants cannot be presumed to make critical decisions without counsel's advice. This is consistent, too, with the rule that defendants have a right to effective assistance of counsel on appeal, even though that cannot in any way be characterized as part of the trial. See, e.g., Halbert v. Michigan, 545 U.S. 605 (2005). The precedents also establish that there exists a right to counsel during sentencing in both noncapital and capital cases. Even though sentencing does not concern the defendant's guilt or innocence, ineffective assistance of counsel during a sentencing hearing can result in *Strickland* prejudice because any amount of additional jail time has Sixth Amendment significance.

The Court, moreover, has not followed a rigid rule that an otherwise fair trial remedies errors not occurring at the trial itself. It has inquired instead whether the trial cured the particular error at issue. Thus, in Vasquez v. Hillery, 474 U.S. 254 (1986), the deliberate exclusion of all African–Americans from a grand jury was prejudicial because a defendant may have been tried on charges that would not have been brought at all by a properly constituted grand jury. By contrast, in United States v. Mechanik, 475 U.S. 66 (1986), the complained-of error was a violation of a grand jury rule meant to ensure probable cause existed to believe a defendant was guilty. A subsequent trial, resulting in a verdict of guilt, cured this error.

In the instant case respondent went to trial rather than accept a plea deal, and it is conceded this was the result of ineffective assistance during the plea negotiation process. Respondent received a more severe sentence at trial, one three and a half times more severe than he likely would have received by pleading guilty. Far from curing the error, the trial caused the injury from the error. Even if the trial itself is free from constitutional flaw, the defendant who goes to trial instead of taking a more favorable plea may be prejudiced from either a conviction on more serious counts or the imposition of a more severe sentence.

Second, petitioner claims this Court refined *Strickland*'s prejudice analysis in Lockhart v. Fretwell, 506 U.S. 364 (1993) to add an additional requirement that the defendant show that ineffective assistance of counsel led to his being denied a substantive or procedural right.... Fretwell could not show *Strickland* prejudice resulting from his attorney's failure to object to the use of a sentencing factor the Eighth Circuit had erroneously (and temporarily) found to be impermissible. Because the objection upon which his ineffective-assistance-of-counsel claim was premised was meritless, Fretwell could not demonstrate an error entitling him to relief. [In situations such as this,] it would be unjust to characterize the likelihood of a different outcome as legitimate "prejudice" because defendants would receive a windfall as a result of the application of an incorrect legal principle or a defense strategy outside the law. Here, however, the injured client seeks relief from counsel's failure to meet a valid legal standard, not from counsel's refusal to violate it....

It is, of course, true that defendants have no right to be offered a plea, nor a federal right that the judge accept it. In the circumstances here, that is beside the point. If no plea offer is made, or a plea deal is accepted by the defendant but rejected by the judge, the issue raised here simply does not arise. Much the same reasoning guides cases that find criminal defendants have a right to effective assistance of counsel in direct appeals even though the Constitution does not require States to provide a system of appellate review at all. As in those cases, when a State opts to act in a field where its action has significant discretionary elements, it must nonetheless act in accord with the dictates of the Constitution.

Third, petitioner seeks to preserve the conviction obtained by the State by arguing that the purpose of the Sixth Amendment is to ensure "the reliability of a conviction following trial." This argument, too, fails to comprehend the full scope of the Sixth Amendment's protections; and it is refuted by precedent. *Strickland* recognized the benchmark for judging any claim of ineffectiveness "must be whether counsel's conduct so undermined the proper functioning of the adversarial process that the trial cannot be relied on as having produced a just result." The goal of a just result is not divorced from the reliability of a conviction; but here the question is not the fairness or reliability of the trial but the fairness and regularity of the processes that preceded it, which caused the defendant to lose benefits he would have received in the ordinary course but for counsel's ineffective assistance.

There are instances, furthermore, where a reliable trial does not foreclose relief when counsel has failed to assert rights that may have altered the outcome. In Kimmelman v. Morrison, 477 U.S. 365 (1986), the Court held that an attorney's failure to timely move to suppress evidence during trial could be grounds for federal habeas relief. The Court rejected the suggestion that the "failure to make a timely request for the exclusion of illegally seized evidence" could not be the basis for a Sixth Amendment violation because the evidence "is typically reliable and often the most probative information bearing on the guilt or innocence of the defendant." The constitutional rights of criminal defendants, the Court observed, "are granted to the innocent and the guilty alike. Consequently, we decline to hold either that the guarantee of effective assistance of counsel belongs solely to the innocent or that it attaches only to matters affecting the determination of actual guilt." The same logic applies here. The fact that respondent is guilty does not mean he was not entitled by the Sixth Amendment to effective assistance or that he suffered no prejudice from his attorney's deficient performance during plea bargaining.

In the end, petitioner's three arguments amount to one general contention: A fair trial wipes clean any deficient performance by defense counsel during plea bargaining. That position ignores the reality that criminal justice today is for the most part a system of pleas, not a system of trials. Ninety-seven percent of federal convictions and ninety-four percent of state convictions are the result of guilty pleas. [The] right to adequate assistance of counsel cannot be defined or enforced without taking account of the central role plea bargaining plays in securing convictions and determining sentences.

C

Even if a defendant shows ineffective assistance of counsel has caused the rejection of a plea leading to a trial and a more severe sentence, there is the question of what constitutes an appropriate remedy. That question must now be addressed.

Sixth Amendment remedies should be tailored to the injury suffered from the constitutional violation and should not unnecessarily infringe on competing interests. Thus, a remedy must neutralize the taint of a constitutional violation while at the same time not grant a windfall to the defendant or needlessly squander the considerable resources the State properly invested in the criminal prosecution.

The specific injury suffered by defendants who decline a plea offer as a result of ineffective assistance of counsel and then receive a greater sentence as a result of trial can come in at least one of two forms. In some cases, the sole advantage a defendant would have received under the plea is a lesser sentence. This is typically the case when the charges that would have been admitted as part of the plea bargain are the same as the charges the defendant was convicted of after trial. In this situation the court may conduct an evidentiary hearing to determine whether the defendant has shown a reasonable probability that but for counsel's errors he would have accepted the plea. If the showing is made, the court may exercise discretion in determining whether the defendant should receive the term of imprisonment the government offered in the plea, the sentence he received at trial, or something in between.

In some situations it may be that resentencing alone will not be full redress for the constitutional injury. If, for example, an offer was for a guilty plea to a count or counts less serious than the ones for which a defendant was convicted after trial, or if a mandatory sentence confines a judge's sentencing discretion after trial, a resentencing based on the conviction at trial may not suffice. In these circumstances, the proper exercise of discretion to remedy the constitutional injury may be to require the prosecution to reoffer the plea proposal. Once this has occurred, the judge can then exercise discretion in deciding whether to vacate the conviction from trial and accept the plea or leave the conviction undisturbed.

In implementing a remedy in both of these situations, the trial court must weigh various factors; and the boundaries of proper discretion need not be defined here. Principles elaborated over time in decisions of state and federal courts, and in statutes and rules, will serve to give more complete guidance as to the factors that should bear upon the exercise of the judge's discretion. At this point, however, it suffices to note two considerations that are of relevance.

First, a court may take account of a defendant's earlier expressed willingness, or unwillingness, to accept responsibility for his or her actions. Second, it is not necessary here to decide as a constitutional rule that a judge is required to prescind (that is to say disregard) any information concerning the crime that was discovered after the plea offer was made. The time continuum makes it difficult to restore the defendant and the prosecution to the precise positions they occupied prior to the rejection of the plea offer, but that baseline can be consulted in finding a remedy that does not require the prosecution to incur the expense of conducting a new trial.

Petitioner argues that implementing a remedy here will open the floodgates to litigation by defendants seeking to unsettle their convictions. Petitioner's concern is misplaced. Courts have recognized claims of this sort for over 30 years, and yet there is no indication that the system is overwhelmed by these types of suits or that defendants are receiving windfalls as a result of strategically timed *Strickland* claims. In addition, the prosecution and the trial courts may adopt some measures to help ensure against late, frivolous, or fabricated claims after a later, less advantageous plea offer has been accepted or after a trial leading to conviction. This, too, will help ensure against meritless claims.

III

The standards for ineffective assistance of counsel when a defendant rejects a plea offer and goes to trial must now be applied to this case. Respondent brings a federal collateral challenge to a state-court conviction. Under AEDPA, a federal court may not grant a petition for a writ of habeas corpus unless the state court's adjudication on the merits was "contrary to, or involved an unreasonable application of, clearly established Federal law, as determined by the Supreme Court of the United States." 28 U.S.C. § 2254(d)(1). A decision is contrary to clearly established law if the state court applies a rule that contradicts the governing law set forth in Supreme Court cases.

[The] Michigan Court of Appeals identified respondent's ineffective-assistance-of-counsel claim but failed to apply *Strickland* to assess it. Rather than applying *Strickland,* the state court simply found that respondent's rejection of the plea was knowing and voluntary. An inquiry into whether the rejection of a plea is knowing and voluntary, however, is not the correct means by which to address a claim of ineffective assistance of counsel.... By failing to apply *Strickland* to assess the ineffective-assistance-of-counsel claim respondent raised, the state court's adjudication was contrary to clearly established federal law....

Respondent has satisfied *Strickland*'s two-part test. [In this case], the fact of deficient performance has been conceded by all parties.... As to prejudice, respondent has shown that but for counsel's deficient performance there is a reasonable probability he and the trial court would have accepted the guilty plea. In addition, as a result of not accepting the plea and being convicted at trial, respondent received a minimum sentence three and one half times greater than he would have received under the plea. The standard for ineffective assistance under *Strickland* has thus been satisfied.

As a remedy, the District Court ordered specific performance of the original plea agreement. The correct remedy in these circumstances, however, is to order the State to reoffer the plea agreement. Presuming respondent accepts the offer, the state trial court can then exercise its discretion in determining whether to vacate the convictions and resentence respondent pursuant to the plea agreement, to vacate only some of the convictions and resentence respondent accordingly, or to leave the convictions and sentence from trial undisturbed. See Mich. Ct. Rule 6.302(C)(3) (2011) ("If there is a plea agreement and its terms provide for the defendant's plea to be made in exchange for a specific sentence disposition or a prosecutorial sentence recommendation, the court may ... reject the agreement"). Today's decision leaves open to the trial court how best to exercise that discretion in all the circumstances of the case....

SCALIA, J., dissenting.[*]

[The] Court today opens a whole new field of constitutionalized criminal procedure: plea-bargaining law. The ordinary criminal process has become too long, too expensive, and unpredictable, in no small part as a consequence of an intricate federal Code of Criminal Procedure imposed on the States by this Court in pursuit of perfect justice. The Court now moves to bring perfection to the alternative in which prosecutors and defendants have sought relief.... And it would be foolish to think that "constitutional" rules governing *counsel*'s behavior will not be followed by rules governing the *prosecution*'s behavior in the plea-bargaining process... Is it constitutional, for example, for the prosecution to withdraw a plea offer that has already been accepted? Or to withdraw an offer before the defense has had adequate time to consider and accept it? Or to make no plea offer at all, even though its case is weak ...?

Anthony Cooper received a full and fair trial, was found guilty of all charges by a unanimous jury, and was given the sentence that the law prescribed. The Court nonetheless concludes that Cooper is entitled to some sort of habeas corpus relief (perhaps) because his attorney's allegedly incompetent advice regarding a plea offer *caused* him to receive a full and fair trial. That conclusion is foreclosed by our precedents.... And the remedy the Court announces—namely, whatever the state trial court in its discretion prescribes, down to and including no remedy at all—is unheard-of and quite absurd for violation of a constitutional right. I respectfully dissent....

This case [raises] relatively straightforward questions about the scope of the right to effective assistance of counsel. Our case law originally derived that right from the Due Process Clause, and its

---

[*] Justice Thomas joined this opinion; Chief Justice Roberts joined all but Part IV of the opinion.

guarantee of a fair trial, but the seminal case of Strickland v. Washington, 466 U.S. 668 (1984), located the right within the Sixth Amendment. As the Court notes, the right to counsel does not begin at trial. It extends to "any stage of the prosecution, formal or informal, in court or out, where counsel's absence might derogate from the accused's right to a fair trial." United States v. Wade, 388 U.S. 218, 226 (1967). Applying that principle, we held that the entry of a guilty plea, whether to a misdemeanor or a felony charge, ranks as a "critical stage" at which the right to counsel adheres. Iowa v. Tovar, 541 U.S. 77, 81 (2004); see also Hill v. Lockhart, 474 U.S. 52 (1985). And it follows from this that *acceptance* of a plea offer is a critical stage. That, and nothing more, is the point of the Court's observation in Padilla v. Kentucky, 130 S. Ct. 1473, 1486 (2010), that "the negotiation of a plea bargain is a critical phase of litigation for purposes of the Sixth Amendment right to effective assistance of counsel." The defendant in *Padilla* had accepted the plea bargain and pleaded guilty, abandoning his right to a fair trial; he was entitled to advice of competent counsel before he did so. The Court has never held that the rule articulated in *Padilla, Tovar,* and *Hill* extends to all aspects of plea negotiations, requiring not just advice of competent counsel before the defendant accepts a plea bargain and pleads guilty, but also the advice of competent counsel before the defendant rejects a plea bargain and stands on his constitutional right to a fair trial. The latter is a vast departure from our past cases, protecting not just the constitutionally prescribed right to a fair adjudication of guilt and punishment, but a judicially invented right to effective plea bargaining.

It is also apparent from *Strickland* that bad plea bargaining has nothing to do with ineffective assistance of counsel in the constitutional sense. *Strickland* explained that in giving meaning to the requirement of effective assistance, "we must take its purpose—to ensure a fair trial—as the guide." Since the right to the effective assistance of counsel is recognized not for its own sake, but because of the effect it has on the ability of the accused to receive a fair trial, the benchmark inquiry in evaluating any claim of ineffective assistance is whether counsel's performance so undermined the proper functioning of the adversarial process that it failed to produce a reliably just result. That is what *Strickland*'s requirement of "prejudice" consists of: Because the right to effective assistance has as its purpose the assurance of a fair trial, the right is not infringed unless counsel's mistakes call into question the basic justice of a defendant's conviction or sentence. That has been, until today, entirely clear.... Impairment of fair trial is how we distinguish between unfortunate attorney error and error of constitutional significance....

It is impossible to conclude discussion of today's extraordinary opinion without commenting upon the remedy it provides for the unconstitutional conviction. It is a remedy unheard-of in American jurisprudence—and, I would be willing to bet, in the jurisprudence of any other country.

The Court requires Michigan to "reoffer the plea agreement" that was rejected because of bad advice from counsel. That would indeed be a powerful remedy—but for the fact that Cooper's acceptance of that reoffered agreement is not conclusive. Astoundingly, "the state trial court can then *exercise its discretion* in determining whether to vacate the convictions and resentence respondent pursuant to the plea agreement, to vacate only some of the convictions and resentence respondent accordingly, *or to leave the convictions and sentence from trial undisturbed.*" (emphasis added)....

To be sure, the Court asserts that there are "factors" which bear upon (and presumably limit) exercise of this discretion—factors that it is not prepared to specify in full, much less assign some determinative weight. "Principles elaborated over time in decisions of state and federal courts, and in statutes and rules" will (in the Court's rosy view) sort all that out. I find it extraordinary that "statutes and rules" can specify the remedy for a criminal defendant's unconstitutional conviction. Or that the remedy for an unconstitutional conviction should *ever* be subject *at all* to a trial judge's discretion. Or, finally, that the remedy could *ever* include no remedy at all.

I suspect that the Court's squeamishness in fashioning a remedy, and the incoherence of what it comes up with, is attributable to its realization, deep down, that there is no real constitutional violation here anyway. The defendant has been fairly tried, lawfully convicted, and properly sentenced, and *any* "remedy" provided for this will do nothing but undo the just results of a fair adversarial process....

In many—perhaps most—countries of the world, American-style plea bargaining is forbidden in cases as serious as this one, even for the purpose of obtaining testimony that enables conviction of a greater malefactor, much less for the purpose of sparing the expense of trial. In Europe, many countries adhere to what they aptly call the "legality principle" by requiring prosecutors to charge all prosecutable offenses, which is typically incompatible with the practice of charge-bargaining. Such a system reflects an admirable belief that the law is the law, and those who break it should pay the penalty provided.

In the United States, we have plea bargaining a-plenty, but until today it has been regarded as a necessary evil. It presents grave risks of prosecutorial overcharging that effectively compels an innocent defendant to avoid massive risk by pleading guilty to a lesser offense; and for guilty defendants it often—perhaps usually—results in a sentence well below what the law prescribes for the actual crime. But even so, we accept plea bargaining because many believe that without it our long and expensive process of criminal trial could not sustain the burden imposed on it, and our system of criminal justice would grind to a halt. Today, however, the Supreme Court of the United States elevates plea bargaining from a necessary evil to a constitutional entitlement....

I am less saddened by the outcome of this case than I am by what it says about this Court's attitude toward criminal justice. The Court today embraces the sporting-chance theory of criminal law, in which the State functions like a conscientious casino-operator, giving each player a fair chance to beat the house, that is, to serve less time than the law says he deserves. And when a player is excluded from the tables, his *constitutional rights* have been violated. I do not subscribe to that theory. No one should, least of all the Justices of the Supreme Court....

Today's decision upends decades of our cases, violates a federal statute, and opens a whole new boutique of constitutional jurisprudence ("plea-bargaining law") without even specifying the remedies the boutique offers. The result in the present case is the undoing of an adjudicatory process that worked *exactly* as it is supposed to. Released felon Anthony Cooper, who shot repeatedly and gravely injured a woman named Kali Mundy, was tried and convicted for his crimes by a jury of his peers, and given a punishment that Michigan's elected representatives have deemed appropriate. Nothing about that result is unfair or unconstitutional. To the contrary, it is wonderfully just, and infinitely superior to the trial-by-bargain that today's opinion affords constitutional status. I respectfully dissent.

Chapter 12

Pretrial Release and Detention

C. Detention of Excludable Aliens and Enemy Combatants

Page 885. Add this material at the end of note 2.

Cf. Ashcroft v. al-Kidd, 131 S. Ct. 2074 (2011) (an arrest of a non-citizen under the federal material support statute was based on individualized suspicion that he was a material witness to a federal crime who would soon disappear unless he was detained; because the government made the showing required by law, the detainee could not invalidate the detention by showing that the true motive for his arrest was a Department of Justice policy to use the statute as a measure to strike preemptively against terrorism suspects).

Chapter 13

Charging

B. Prosecutorial Screening

3. Private Prosecution

Page 932. Insert the following material at the end of note 3.

See In re Richland County Magistrate's Court, 699 S.E.2d 161 (S.C. 2010) (state law that authorizes non-lawyers to represent business in civil actions in magistrate's does not extend to non-lawyers prosecuting misdemeanor charges on behalf of business).

4. Selection of Charges and System

Page 952. Insert the following material at the end of note 2.

See State v. B.B., 17 A.3d 30 (Conn. 2011) (failure to hold a hearing prior to transfer does not constitute a denial of due process; juvenile's liberty interest is vindicated by a hearing in adult court).

5.   Selective Prosecution

Page 961. Insert the following material at the end of note 1.

See also In re D.B., 950 N.E.2d 528 (Ohio 2011) (application of statutory rape provision to a child under age 13 who engages in sexual conduct with another child under age 13 violates the Equal Protection Clause mandate that persons similarly circumstanced be treated alike).

Chapter 15

Discovery and Speedy Trial

A. Discovery

1. Prosecution Disclosure of Exculpatory Information

Page 1050. Insert the following material at the end of note 3.

See Smith v. Cain, 132 S. Ct. 627 (2012) (statements by the eyewitness contradicting his testimony was material for *Brady* purposes because testimony was the only evidence linking defendant to the crime, and the eyewitness's undisclosed statements contradicted his testimony).

Page 1052. Insert the following material at the end of note 8.

However clear-cut the *Brady* violation may be, monetary damages for wronged defendants are extremely limited under the federal civil rights statute, 42 U.S.C. §1983. In Connick v. Thompson, 131 S. Ct. 1350 (2011), the Supreme Court overturned a jury verdict for $14 million against the District Attorney of Orleans Parish, Harry Connick. The plaintiff, John Thompson, was wrongly convicted of robbery and capital murder after prosecutors knowingly failed to disclose to defense attorneys the existence of a blood test confirming the innocence of the defendant, as well as tape recordings that impeached the credibility of key prosecution witnesses. He spent 18 years in prison (and 14 years on death row) before his investigator discovered the evidence and a reviewing court vacated his conviction. The District Attorney's office retried Thompson for the murder despite the exculpatory evidence, but the jury acquitted him.

Recovery in tort against the individual prosecutors was impossible because of absolute prosecutorial immunity. According to Justice Thomas, recovery against the district attorney's office was also barred under the federal statute because there was no adequate proof that the *Brady* violation resulted from a "policy or custom" of the office. A failure by the office supervisors to train prosecutors about their discovery obligations would amount to a Section 1983 violation only if that failure reflected a "deliberate indifference" to the violation of defendants' rights. The court characterized the failure of multiple prosecutors over many years to disclose the evidence in the case as a "single violation," and therefore not enough to prove the necessary pattern or practice. Although other prosecutors in the office had committed *Brady* violations during the ten years prior to Thompson's trial (leading to four reversals of convictions in the appellate courts), Justice Thomas declared that those other violations were different in character and unrelated to the violation in Thompson's case. The *Brady* violations in the other cases, the Court explained, did not involve the failure to disclose physical evidence or crime lab reports.

Based on this holding, it appears that monetary damages under Section 1983 will be available only in cases when plaintiffs can prove multiple closely-related *Brady* violations in a single office over a short period of time. Given the difficulty of uncovering even a single *Brady* violation, such damages will prove to be a practical impossibility. Will any civil plaintiff in any case ever meet this standard, or ever even obtain discovery on the question? Cf. United States v. Armstrong, 517 U.S. 456 (1996) (establishing an extremely demanding standard for obtaining discovery on selective prosecution claims).

Chapter 16

Pleas and Bargains

C. Validity of Individual Plea Bargains

1. Lack of Knowledge

Page 1162. Place this material at the end of note 3.

Missouri v. Galin Frye
132 S. Ct. 1399 (2012)

KENNEDY, J.[*]
... This case arises in the context of claimed ineffective assistance that led to the lapse of a prosecution offer of a plea bargain, a proposal that offered terms more lenient than the terms of the guilty plea entered later. The initial question is whether the constitutional right to counsel extends to the negotiation and consideration of plea offers that lapse or are rejected. If there is a right to effective assistance with respect to those offers, a further question is what a defendant must demonstrate in order to show that prejudice resulted from counsel's deficient performance....

I

In August 2007, respondent Galin Frye was charged with driving with a revoked license. Frye had been convicted for that offense on three

---

[*] Justices Ginsburg, Breyer, Sotomayor, and Kagan joined this opinion.

other occasions, so the State of Missouri charged him with a class D felony, which carries a maximum term of imprisonment of four years.

On November 15, the prosecutor sent a letter to Frye's counsel offering a choice of two plea bargains. The prosecutor first offered to recommend a 3-year sentence if there was a guilty plea to the felony charge, without a recommendation regarding probation but with a recommendation that Frye serve 10 days in jail as so-called "shock" time. The second offer was to reduce the charge to a misdemeanor and, if Frye pleaded guilty to it, to recommend a 90–day sentence. The misdemeanor charge of driving with a revoked license carries a maximum term of imprisonment of one year. The letter stated both offers would expire on December 28. Frye's attorney did not advise Frye that the offers had been made. The offers expired.

Frye's preliminary hearing was scheduled for January 4, 2008. On December 30, 2007, less than a week before the hearing, Frye was again arrested for driving with a revoked license. At the January 4 hearing, Frye waived his right to a preliminary hearing on the charge arising from the August 2007 arrest. He pleaded not guilty at a subsequent arraignment but then changed his plea to guilty. There was no underlying plea agreement. The state trial court accepted Frye's guilty plea. The prosecutor recommended a 3-year sentence, made no recommendation regarding probation, and requested 10 days shock time in jail. The trial judge sentenced Frye to three years in prison.

Frye filed for post-conviction relief in state court. He alleged his counsel's failure to inform him of the prosecution's plea offer denied him the effective assistance of counsel. At an evidentiary hearing, Frye testified he would have entered a guilty plea to the misdemeanor had he known about the offer.

A state court denied the post-conviction motion, but the Missouri Court of Appeals reversed. It determined that Frye met both of the requirements for showing a Sixth Amendment violation under *Strickland*. First, the court determined Frye's counsel's performance was deficient because the "record is void of any evidence of any effort by trial counsel to communicate the Offer to Frye during the Offer window." The court next concluded Frye had shown his counsel's deficient performance caused him prejudice because "Frye pled guilty to a felony instead of a misdemeanor and was subject to a maximum sentence of four years instead of one year."

To implement a remedy for the violation, the court deemed Frye's guilty plea withdrawn and remanded to allow Frye either to insist on a trial or to plead guilty to any offense the prosecutor deemed it appropriate to charge. This Court granted certiorari.

II A

It is well settled that the right to the effective assistance of counsel applies to certain steps before trial. The Sixth Amendment guarantees a defendant the right to have counsel present at all "critical" stages of the criminal proceedings. Critical stages include arraignments, post-indictment interrogations, post-indictment lineups, and the entry of a guilty plea.

With respect to the right to effective counsel in plea negotiations, a proper beginning point is to discuss two cases from this Court considering the role of counsel in advising a client about a plea offer and an ensuing guilty plea: Hill v. Lockhart, 474 U.S. 52 (1985); and Padilla v. Kentucky, 559 U.S. ___ (2010).

Hill established that claims of ineffective assistance of counsel in the plea bargain context are governed by the two-part test set forth in *Strickland....* In *Hill,* the decision turned on the second part of the *Strickland* test. There, a defendant who had entered a guilty plea claimed his counsel had misinformed him of the amount of time he would have to serve before he became eligible for parole. But the defendant had not alleged that, even if adequate advice and assistance had been given, he would have elected to plead not guilty and proceed to trial. Thus, the Court found that no prejudice from the inadequate advice had been shown or alleged.

In *Padilla,* the Court again discussed the duties of counsel in advising a client with respect to a plea offer that leads to a guilty plea. *Padilla* held that a guilty plea, based on a plea offer, should be set aside because counsel misinformed the defendant of the immigration consequences of the conviction. The Court made clear that "the negotiation of a plea bargain is a critical phase of litigation for purposes of the Sixth Amendment right to effective assistance of counsel." It also rejected the argument made by petitioner in this case that a knowing and voluntary plea supersedes errors by defense counsel.

In the case now before the Court the State, as petitioner, points out that the legal question presented is different from that in *Hill* and *Padilla.* In those cases the claim was that the prisoner's plea of guilty was invalid because counsel had provided incorrect advice pertinent to the plea. In the instant case, by contrast, the guilty plea that was accepted, and the plea proceedings concerning it in court, were all based on accurate advice and information from counsel. The challenge is not to the advice pertaining to the plea that was accepted but rather to the course of legal representation that preceded it with respect to other potential pleas and plea offers.

To give further support to its contention that the instant case is in a category different from what the Court considered in *Hill* and *Padilla,* the State urges that there is no right to a plea offer or a plea bargain in any event. It claims Frye therefore was not deprived of any legal benefit to which he was entitled. Under this view, any wrongful or mistaken action of counsel with respect to earlier plea offers is beside the point.

The State is correct to point out that *Hill* and *Padilla* concerned whether there was ineffective assistance leading to acceptance of a plea offer, a process involving a formal court appearance with the defendant and all counsel present. Before a guilty plea is entered the defendant's understanding of the plea and its consequences can be established on the record. This affords the State substantial protection against later claims that the plea was the result of inadequate advice. At the plea entry proceedings the trial court and all counsel have the opportunity to establish on the record that the defendant understands the process that led to any offer, the advantages and disadvantages of accepting it, and the sentencing consequences or possibilities that will ensue once a conviction is entered based upon the plea. *Hill* and *Padilla* both illustrate that, nevertheless, there may be instances when claims of ineffective assistance can arise after the conviction is entered. Still, the State, and the trial court itself, have had a substantial opportunity to guard against this contingency by establishing at the plea entry proceeding that the defendant has been given proper advice or, if the advice received appears to have been inadequate, to remedy that deficiency before the plea is accepted and the conviction entered.

When a plea offer has lapsed or been rejected, however, no formal court proceedings are involved. This underscores that the plea-bargaining process is often in flux, with no clear standards or timelines and with no judicial supervision of the discussions between prosecution and defense. Indeed, discussions between client and defense counsel are privileged. So the prosecution has little or no notice if something may be amiss and perhaps no capacity to intervene in any event. And, as noted, the State insists there is no right to receive a plea offer. For all these reasons, the

114

State contends, it is unfair to subject it to the consequences of defense counsel's inadequacies, especially when the opportunities for a full and fair trial, or, as here, for a later guilty plea albeit on less favorable terms, are preserved.

The State's contentions are neither illogical nor without some persuasive force, yet they do not suffice to overcome a simple reality. Ninety-seven percent of federal convictions and ninety-four percent of state convictions are the result of guilty pleas. The reality is that plea bargains have become so central to the administration of the criminal justice system that defense counsel have responsibilities in the plea bargain process, responsibilities that must be met to render the adequate assistance of counsel that the Sixth Amendment requires in the criminal process at critical stages. Because ours is for the most part a system of pleas, not a system of trials, it is insufficient simply to point to the guarantee of a fair trial as a backstop that inoculates any errors in the pretrial process. "To a large extent ... horse trading [between prosecutor and defense counsel] determines who goes to jail and for how long. That is what plea bargaining is. It is not some adjunct to the criminal justice system; it *is* the criminal justice system." Scott & Stuntz, Plea Bargaining as Contract, 101 Yale L. J. 1909, 1912 (1992). In today's criminal justice system, therefore, the negotiation of a plea bargain, rather than the unfolding of a trial, is almost always the critical point for a defendant.

To note the prevalence of plea bargaining is not to criticize it. The potential to conserve valuable prosecutorial resources and for defendants to admit their crimes and receive more favorable terms at sentencing means that a plea agreement can benefit both parties. In order that these benefits can be realized, however, criminal defendants require effective counsel during plea negotiations....

B

The inquiry then becomes how to define the duty and responsibilities of defense counsel in the plea bargain process. This is a difficult question. The art of negotiation is at least as nuanced as the art of trial advocacy and it presents questions farther removed from immediate judicial supervision. Bargaining is, by its nature, defined to a substantial degree by personal style. The alternative courses and tactics in negotiation are so individual that it may be neither prudent nor practicable to try to elaborate or define detailed standards for the proper discharge of defense counsel's participation in the process.

This case presents neither the necessity nor the occasion to define the duties of defense counsel in those respects, however. Here the question is whether defense counsel has the duty to communicate the terms of a formal offer to accept a plea on terms and conditions that may result in a lesser sentence, a conviction on lesser charges, or both.

This Court now holds that, as a general rule, defense counsel has the duty to communicate formal offers from the prosecution to accept a plea on terms and conditions that may be favorable to the accused. Any exceptions to that rule need not be explored here, for the offer was a formal one with a fixed expiration date. When defense counsel allowed the offer to expire without advising the defendant or allowing him to consider it, defense counsel did not render the effective assistance the Constitution requires.

Though the standard for counsel's performance is not determined solely by reference to codified standards of professional practice, these standards can be important guides. The American Bar Association recommends defense counsel "promptly communicate and explain to the defendant all plea offers made by the prosecuting attorney," ABA Standards for Criminal Justice, Pleas of Guilty 14–3.2(a) (3d ed. 1999), and this standard has been adopted by numerous state and federal courts over the last 30 years. The standard for prompt communication and consultation is also set out in state bar professional standards for attorneys.

The prosecution and the trial courts may adopt some measures to help ensure against late, frivolous, or fabricated claims after a later, less advantageous plea offer has been accepted or after a trial leading to conviction with resulting harsh consequences. First, the fact of a formal offer means that its terms and its processing can be documented so that what took place in the negotiation process becomes more clear if some later inquiry turns on the conduct of earlier pretrial negotiations. Second, States may elect to follow rules that all offers must be in writing, again to ensure against later misunderstandings or fabricated charges. Third, formal offers can be made part of the record at any subsequent plea proceeding or before a trial on the merits, all to ensure that a defendant has been fully advised before those further proceedings commence. At least one State [Arizona] often follows a similar procedure before trial.

Here defense counsel did not communicate the formal offers to the defendant. As a result of that deficient performance, the offers lapsed.

Under *Strickland,* the question then becomes what, if any, prejudice resulted from the breach of duty.

C

To show prejudice from ineffective assistance of counsel where a plea offer has lapsed or been rejected because of counsel's deficient performance, defendants must demonstrate a reasonable probability they would have accepted the earlier plea offer had they been afforded effective assistance of counsel. Defendants must also demonstrate a reasonable probability the plea would have been entered without the prosecution canceling it or the trial court refusing to accept it, if they had the authority to exercise that discretion under state law. To establish prejudice in this instance, it is necessary to show a reasonable probability that the end result of the criminal process would have been more favorable by reason of a plea to a lesser charge or a sentence of less prison time.

This application of *Strickland* to the instances of an uncommunicated, lapsed plea does nothing to alter the standard laid out in *Hill.* In cases where a defendant complains that ineffective assistance led him to accept a plea offer as opposed to proceeding to trial, the defendant will have to show "a reasonable probability that, but for counsel's errors, he would not have pleaded guilty and would have insisted on going to trial." *Hill,* 474 U.S., at 59. *Hill* was correctly decided and applies in the context in which it arose. *Hill* does not, however, provide the sole means for demonstrating prejudice arising from the deficient performance of counsel during plea negotiations. Unlike the defendant in *Hill,* Frye argues that with effective assistance he would have accepted an earlier plea offer (limiting his sentence to one year in prison) as opposed to entering an open plea (exposing him to a maximum sentence of four years' imprisonment). In a case, such as this, where a defendant pleads guilty to less favorable terms and claims that ineffective assistance of counsel caused him to miss out on a more favorable earlier plea offer, *Strickland*'s inquiry into whether "the result of the proceeding would have been different" requires looking not at whether the defendant would have proceeded to trial absent ineffective assistance but whether he would have accepted the offer to plead pursuant to the terms earlier proposed.

In order to complete a showing of *Strickland* prejudice, defendants who have shown a reasonable probability they would have accepted the earlier plea offer must also show that, if the prosecution had the discretion to cancel it or if the trial court had the discretion to refuse to accept it, there is a reasonable probability neither the prosecution nor the trial court would have prevented the offer from being accepted or implemented. This further showing is of particular importance because a defendant has no right to be offered a plea, nor a federal right that the judge accept it. In at least some States, including Missouri, it appears the prosecution has some discretion to cancel a plea agreement to which the defendant has agreed. The Federal Rules, some state rules including in Missouri, and this Court's precedents give trial courts some leeway to accept or reject plea agreements. It can be assumed that in most jurisdictions prosecutors and judges are familiar with the boundaries of acceptable plea bargains and sentences. So in most instances it should not be difficult to make an objective assessment as to whether or not a particular fact or intervening circumstance would suffice, in the normal course, to cause prosecutorial withdrawal or judicial nonapproval of a plea bargain. The determination that there is or is not a reasonable probability that the outcome of the proceeding would have been different absent counsel's errors can be conducted within that framework.

III

These standards must be applied to the instant case. As regards the deficient performance prong of *Strickland,* … it is evident that Frye's attorney did not make a meaningful attempt to inform the defendant of a written plea offer before the offer expired. The Missouri Court of Appeals was correct that "counsel's representation fell below an objective standard of reasonableness."

The Court of Appeals erred, however, in articulating the precise standard for prejudice in this context. As noted, a defendant in Frye's position must show not only a reasonable probability that he would have accepted the lapsed plea but also a reasonable probability that the prosecution would have adhered to the agreement and that it would have been accepted by the trial court. Frye can show he would have accepted the offer, but there is strong reason to doubt the prosecution and the trial court would have permitted the plea bargain to become final.

There appears to be a reasonable probability Frye would have accepted the prosecutor's original offer of a plea bargain if the offer had been communicated to him, because he pleaded guilty to a more serious charge, with no promise of a sentencing recommendation from the prosecutor. It may be that in some cases defendants must show more than just a guilty plea to a charge or sentence harsher than the original offer. For example, revelations between plea offers about the strength of the prosecution's case may make a late decision to plead guilty insufficient to demonstrate, without further evidence, that the defendant would have pleaded guilty to an earlier, more generous plea offer if his counsel had reported it to him. Here, however, that is not the case. The Court of Appeals did not err in finding Frye's acceptance of the less favorable plea offer indicated that he would have accepted the earlier (and more favorable) offer had he been apprised of it; and there is no need to address here the showings that might be required in other cases.

The Court of Appeals failed, however, to require Frye to show that the first plea offer, if accepted by Frye, would have been adhered to by the prosecution and accepted by the trial court. Whether the prosecution and trial court are required to do so is a matter of state law, and it is not the place of this Court to settle those matters. The Court has established the minimum requirements of the Sixth Amendment as interpreted in *Strickland,* and States have the discretion to add procedural protections under state law if they choose. A State may choose to preclude the prosecution from withdrawing a plea offer once it has been accepted or perhaps to preclude a trial court from rejecting a plea bargain. In Missouri, it appears a plea offer once accepted by the defendant can be withdrawn without recourse by the prosecution. The extent of the trial court's discretion in Missouri to reject a plea agreement appears to be in some doubt.

We remand for the Missouri Court of Appeals to consider these state-law questions, because they bear on the federal question of *Strickland* prejudice. If, as the Missouri court stated here, the prosecutor could have canceled the plea agreement, and if Frye fails to show a reasonable probability the prosecutor would have adhered to the agreement, there is no *Strickland* prejudice. Likewise, if the trial court could have refused to accept the plea agreement, and if Frye fails to show a reasonable probability the trial court would have accepted the plea, there is no *Strickland* prejudice. In this case, given Frye's new offense for driving without a license on December 30, 2007, there is reason to doubt that the prosecution would have adhered to the agreement or that the trial court would have accepted it at the January 4, 2008, hearing, unless they were required by state law to do so....

SCALIA, J., dissenting.[*]

This is a companion case to Lafler v. Cooper, 132 S. Ct. 1376 (2012). The principal difference between the cases is that the fairness of the defendant's conviction in *Lafler* was established by a full trial and jury verdict, whereas Frye's conviction here was established by his own admission of guilt, received by the court after the usual colloquy that assured it was voluntary and truthful. In *Lafler* all that could be said (and as I discuss there it was quite enough) is that the *fairness* of the conviction was clear, though a unanimous jury finding beyond a reasonable doubt can sometimes be wrong. Here it can be said not only that the process was fair, but that the defendant acknowledged the correctness of his conviction. Thus, as far as the reasons for my dissent are concerned, this is an *a fortiori* case....

Galin Frye's attorney failed to inform him about a plea offer, and Frye ultimately pleaded guilty without the benefit of a deal. Counsel's mistake did not deprive Frye of any substantive or procedural right; only of the opportunity to accept a plea bargain to which he had no entitlement in the first place. So little entitlement that, had he known of and accepted the bargain, the prosecution would have been able to withdraw it right up to the point that his guilty plea pursuant to the bargain was accepted.

[In future cases] it will not be so clear that counsel's plea-bargaining skills, which must now meet a constitutional minimum, are adequate.... What if an attorney's personal style is to establish a reputation as a hard bargainer by, for example, advising clients to proceed to trial rather than accept anything but the most favorable plea offers? It seems inconceivable that a lawyer could compromise his client's *constitutional rights* so that he can secure better deals for other clients in the future; does a hard-bargaining personal style now violate the Sixth Amendment? [This case presents] the necessity of confronting the serious difficulties that will be created by constitutionalization of the plea-bargaining process. It will not do simply to announce that they will be solved in the sweet by-and-by....

Prejudice is to be determined, the Court tells us, by a process of retrospective crystal-ball gazing posing as legal analysis. First of all, of course, we must estimate whether the defendant *would have accepted* the earlier plea bargain. Here that seems an easy question, but as the Court acknowledges, it will not always be. Next, since Missouri, like other

---

[*] Chief Justice Roberts and Justices Thomas and Alito joined this opinion.

States, permits accepted plea offers to be withdrawn by the prosecution (a reality which alone should suffice, one would think, to demonstrate that Frye had no entitlement to the plea bargain), we must estimate whether the prosecution *would have withdrawn* the plea offer. And finally, we must estimate whether the trial court *would have approved* the plea agreement. These last two estimations may seem easy in the present case, since Frye committed a new infraction before the hearing at which the agreement would have been presented; but they assuredly will not be easy in the mine run of cases....

Virtually no cases deal with the standards for a prosecutor's withdrawal from a plea agreement beyond stating the general rule that a prosecutor may withdraw any time prior to, but not after, the entry of a guilty plea or other action constituting detrimental reliance on the defendant's part. And cases addressing trial courts' authority to accept or reject plea agreements almost universally observe that a trial court enjoys broad discretion in this regard. Of course after today's opinions there will be cases galore.... Whatever the "boundaries" ultimately devised (if that were possible), a vast amount of discretion will still remain, and it is extraordinary to make a defendant's constitutional rights depend upon a series of retrospective mind-readings as to how that discretion, in prosecutors and trial judges, *would have been* exercised.

The plea-bargaining process is a subject worthy of regulation, since it is the means by which most criminal convictions are obtained. It happens not to be, however, a subject covered by the Sixth Amendment, which is concerned not with the fairness of bargaining but with the fairness of conviction. [In this case] the Court's sledge may require the reversal of perfectly valid, eminently just, convictions. A legislature could solve the problems presented by these cases in a much more precise and efficient manner. It might begin, for example, by penalizing the attorneys who made such grievous errors. That type of sub-constitutional remedy is not available to the Court, which is limited to penalizing (almost) everyone else by reversing valid convictions or sentences. Because that result is inconsistent with the Sixth Amendment and decades of our precedent, I respectfully dissent.

Chapter 17

Decisionmakers at Trial

C. Jury Deliberations and Verdicts

1. Deadlocked Juries

Page 1250. Place this material before the notes.

See Blueford v. Arkansas, 132 S. Ct. 2044 (2012) (second trial after mistrial not barred by double jeopardy; defendant in first trial was charged with capital murder and lesser-included homicide offenses, and jury was given verdict forms that allowed them to acquit of all charges or to convict of one charge).

Chapter 18

Witnesses and Proof

B. *Confrontation of Witnesses*

2. Unavailable Prosecution Witnesses

Page 1322. Place this material after *Crawford v. Washington*.

Crawford v. Washington was a constitutional earthquake, and the aftershocks continue to be felt in cases before the United States Supreme Court, and throughout state and federal courts. *Crawford* has both sharpened and blurred the lines between the constitutional limits on the admission of evidence and the law and rules of evidence. With later decisions *Crawford* has demonstrated very complex doctrinal, policy and historical dimensions. All of these tensions are fully evident in the most recent United States Supreme Court effort at line-drawing under *Crawford* in the third major post-*Crawford* case to address the general issue of when testimony by expert witnesses is testimonial or otherwise triggers (or does not trigger) the protection of the confrontation clause.

Sandy Williams v. Illinois
132 S. Ct. 2221 (2012)

ALITO, J.[*]

In this case, we decide whether Crawford v. Washington, 541 U.S. 36 (2004), precludes an expert witness from testifying in a manner that has long been allowed under the law of evidence. Specifically, does *Crawford* bar an expert from expressing an opinion based on facts about a case that have been made known to the expert but about which the expert is not competent to testify? We also decide whether *Crawford* substantially impedes the ability of prosecutors to introduce DNA evidence and thus may effectively relegate the prosecution in some cases to reliance on older, less reliable forms of proof.

In petitioner's bench trial for rape, the prosecution called an expert who testified that a DNA profile produced by an outside laboratory, Cellmark, matched a profile produced by the state police lab using a sample of petitioner's blood. On direct examination, the expert testified that Cellmark was an accredited laboratory and that Cellmark provided the police with a DNA profile. The expert also explained the notations on documents admitted as business records, stating that, according to the records, vaginal swabs taken from the victim were sent to and received back from Cellmark. The expert made no other statement that was offered for the purpose of identifying the sample of biological material used in deriving the profile or for the purpose of establishing how Cellmark handled or tested the sample. Nor did the expert vouch for the accuracy of the profile that Cellmark produced. Nevertheless, petitioner contends that the expert's testimony violated the Confrontation Clause as interpreted in *Crawford*.

Petitioner's main argument is that the expert went astray when she referred to the DNA profile provided by Cellmark as having been produced from semen found on the victim's vaginal swabs. But both the Illinois Appellate Court and the Illinois Supreme Court found that this statement was not admitted for the truth of the matter asserted, and it is settled that the Confrontation Clause does not bar the admission of such statements. For more than 200 years, the law of evidence has permitted the sort of testimony that was given by the expert in this case. Under

---

[*] [Chief Justice Roberts, Justice Kennedy and Justice Breyer joined this opinion. — EDS.]

settled evidence law, an expert may express an opinion that is based on facts that the expert assumes, but does not know, to be true. It is then up to the party who calls the expert to introduce other evidence establishing the facts assumed by the expert. While it was once the practice for an expert who based an opinion on assumed facts to testify in the form of an answer to a hypothetical question, modern practice does not demand this formality and, in appropriate cases, permits an expert to explain the facts on which his or her opinion is based without testifying to the truth of those facts. See Fed. Rule Evid. 703. That is precisely what occurred in this case, and we should not lightly [sweep] away an accepted rule governing the admission of scientific evidence.

We now conclude that this form of expert testimony does not violate the Confrontation Clause because that provision has no application to out-of-court statements that are not offered to prove the truth of the matter asserted. When an expert testifies for the prosecution in a criminal case, the defendant has the opportunity to cross-examine the expert about any statements that are offered for their truth. Out-of-court statements that are related by the expert solely for the purpose of explaining the assumptions on which that opinion rests are not offered for their truth and thus fall outside the scope of the Confrontation Clause. Applying this rule to the present case, we conclude that the expert's testimony did not violate the Sixth Amendment.

As a second, independent basis for our decision, we also conclude that even if the report produced by Cellmark had been admitted into evidence, there would have been no Confrontation Clause violation. The Cellmark report is very different from the sort of extrajudicial statements, such as affidavits, depositions, prior testimony, and confessions, that the Confrontation Clause was originally understood to reach. The report was produced before any suspect was identified. The report was sought not for the purpose of obtaining evidence to be used against petitioner, who was not even under suspicion at the time, but for the purpose of finding a rapist who was on the loose. And the profile that Cellmark provided was not inherently inculpatory. On the contrary, a DNA profile is evidence that tends to exculpate all but one of the more than 7 billion people in the world today. The use of DNA evidence to exonerate persons who have been wrongfully accused or convicted is well known. If DNA profiles could not be introduced without calling the technicians who participated in the preparation of the profile, economic pressures would encourage prosecutors to forgo DNA testing and rely instead on older forms of evidence, such as eyewitness identification, that are less reliable. The Confrontation Clause does not mandate such an undesirable development. This conclusion will not prejudice any defendant who really wishes to probe the reliability of the DNA testing done in a particular case because those who participated in the testing may always be subpoenaed by the defense and questioned at trial.

I A

On February 10, 2000, in Chicago, Illinois, a young woman, L.J., was abducted while she was walking home from work. The perpetrator forced her into his car and raped her, then robbed her of her money and other personal items and pushed her out into the street. L.J. ran home and reported the attack to her mother, who called the police. An ambulance took L.J. to the hospital, where doctors treated her wounds and took a blood sample and vaginal swabs for a sexual-assault kit. A Chicago Police detective collected the kit, labeled it with an inventory number, and sent it under seal to the Illinois State Police (ISP) lab.

At the ISP lab, a forensic scientist received the sealed kit. He conducted a chemical test that confirmed the presence of semen on the vaginal swabs, and he then resealed the kit and placed it in a secure evidence freezer.

During the period in question, the ISP lab often sent biological samples to Cellmark Diagnostics Laboratory in Germantown, Maryland, for DNA testing. There was evidence that the ISP lab sent L.J.'s vaginal swabs to Cellmark for testing and that Cellmark sent back a report containing a male DNA profile produced from semen taken from those swabs. At this time, petitioner was not under suspicion for L.J.'s rape.

Sandra Lambatos, a forensic specialist at the ISP lab, conducted a computer search to see if the Cellmark profile matched any of the entries in the state DNA database. The computer showed a match to a profile produced by the lab from a sample of petitioner's blood that had been taken after he was arrested on unrelated charges on August 3, 2000.

On April 17, 2001, the police conducted a lineup at which L.J. identified petitioner as her assailant. Petitioner was then indicted for aggravated criminal sexual assault, aggravated kidnaping, and aggravated robbery. In lieu of a jury trial, petitioner chose to be tried before a state judge.

B

Petitioner's bench trial began in April 2006. In open court, L.J. again identified petitioner as her attacker. The State also offered three expert forensic witnesses to link petitioner to the crime through his DNA. First, Brian Hapack, an ISP forensic scientist, testified that he had confirmed the presence of semen on the vaginal swabs taken from L.J. by performing an acid phosphatase test. After performing this test, he testified, he resealed the evidence and left it in a secure freezer at the ISP lab.

Second, Karen Abbinanti, a state forensic analyst, testified that she had used Polymerase Chain Reaction (PCR) and Short Tandem Repeat (STR) techniques to develop a DNA profile from a blood sample that had been drawn from petitioner after he was arrested in August 2000. She also stated that she had entered petitioner's DNA profile into the state forensic database.

Third, the State offered Sandra Lambatos as an expert witness in forensic biology and forensic DNA analysis. On direct examination, Lambatos testified about the general process of using the PCR and STR techniques to generate DNA profiles from forensic samples such as blood and semen. She then described how these DNA profiles could be matched to an individual based on the individual's unique genetic code. In making a comparison between two DNA profiles, Lambatos stated, it is a "commonly accepted" practice within the scientific community for "one DNA expert to rely on the records of another DNA expert." Lambatos also testified that Cellmark was an "accredited crime lab" and that, in her experience, the ISP lab routinely sent evidence samples via Federal Express to Cellmark for DNA testing in order to expedite the testing process and to "reduce [the lab's] backlog." To keep track of evidence samples and preserve the chain of custody, Lambatos stated, she and other analysts relied on sealed shipping containers and labeled shipping manifests, and she added that experts in her field regularly relied on such protocols.

Lambatos was shown shipping manifests that were admitted into evidence as business records, and she explained what they indicated, namely, that the ISP lab had sent L.J.'s vaginal swabs to Cellmark, and that Cellmark had sent them back, along with a deduced male DNA profile. The prosecutor asked Lambatos whether there was "a computer match" between "the male DNA profile found in semen from the vaginal swabs of [L.J.]" and the "male DNA profile that had been identified" from petitioner's blood sample.

129

The defense attorney objected to this question for "lack of foundation," arguing that the prosecution had offered "no evidence with regard to any testing that's been done to generate a DNA profile by another lab to be testified to by this witness."

The prosecutor responded: "I'm not getting at what another lab did." Rather, she said, she was simply asking Lambatos about "her own testing based on [DNA] information" that she had received from Cellmark. The trial judge agreed, noting, "If she says she didn't do her own testing and she relied on a test of another lab and she's testifying to that, we will see what she's going to say."

The prosecutor then proceeded, asking Lambatos, "Did you compare the semen that had been identified by Brian Hapack from the vaginal swabs of [L.J.] to the male DNA profile that had been identified by Karen [Abbinanti] from the blood of [petitioner]?"

Lambatos answered "Yes." Defense counsel lodged an objection "to the form of the question," but the trial judge overruled it. Lambatos then testified that, based on her own comparison of the two DNA profiles, she "concluded that [petitioner] cannot be excluded as a possible source of the semen identified in the vaginal swabs," and that the probability of the profile's appearing in the general population was "1 in 8.7 quadrillion black, 1 in 390 quadrillion white, or 1 in 109 quadrillion Hispanic unrelated individuals." Asked whether she would "call this a match to [petitioner]," Lambatos answered yes, again over defense counsel's objection.

The Cellmark report itself was neither admitted into evidence nor shown to the factfinder. Lambatos did not quote or read from the report; nor did she identify it as the source of any of the opinions she expressed.

On cross-examination, Lambatos confirmed that she did not conduct or observe any of the testing on the vaginal swabs, and that her testimony relied on the DNA profile produced by Cellmark. She stated that she trusted Cellmark to do reliable work because it was an accredited lab, but she admitted she had not seen any of the calibrations or work that Cellmark had done in deducing a male DNA profile from the vaginal swabs.

Asked whether the DNA sample might have been degraded before Cellmark analyzed it, Lambatos answered that, while degradation was technically possible, she strongly doubted it had occurred in this case. She gave two reasons. First, the ISP lab likely would have noticed the degradation before sending the evidence off to Cellmark. Second, and more important, Lambatos also noted that the data making up the DNA profile would exhibit certain telltale signs if it had been deduced from a degraded sample: The visual representation of the DNA sequence would exhibit "specific patterns" of degradation, and she "didn't see any evidence" of that from looking at the profile that Cellmark produced.

When Lambatos finished testifying, the defense moved to exclude her testimony "with regards to testing done by [Cellmark]" based on the Confrontation Clause. Defense counsel argued that there was "no evidence with regards to ... any work done by [Cellmark] to justify testimony coming into this case with regard to their analysis." Thus, while defense counsel objected to and sought the exclusion of Lambatos' testimony insofar as it implicated events at the Cellmark lab, defense counsel did not object to or move for the exclusion of any other portion of Lambatos' testimony, including statements regarding the contents of the shipment sent to or received back from Cellmark.

The prosecution responded that petitioner's Confrontation Clause rights were satisfied because he had the opportunity to cross-examine the expert who had testified that there was a match between the DNA profiles produced by Cellmark and Abbinanti. Invoking Illinois Rule of Evidence 703,[1] the prosecutor argued that an expert is allowed to disclose the facts on which the expert's opinion is based even if the expert is not competent to testify to those underlying facts. She further argued that any deficiency in the foundation for the expert's opinion "doesn't go to the admissibility of [that] testimony," but instead "goes to the weight of the testimony."

The trial judge agreed with the prosecution and stated that "the issue is ... what weight do you give the test, not do you exclude it." Accordingly, the judge stated that he would not exclude Lambatos' testimony, which was "based on her own independent testing of the data received from [Cellmark]."

The trial court found petitioner guilty of the charges against him. The state court of appeals affirmed in relevant part, concluding that Lambatos' testimony did not violate petitioner's confrontation rights because the Cellmark report was not offered into evidence to prove the

---

[1] Consistent with the Federal Rules, Illinois Rule of Evidence 703 provides as follows: "The facts or data in the particular case upon which an expert bases an opinion or inference may be those perceived by or made known to the expert at or before the hearing. If of a type reasonably relied upon by experts in the particular field in forming opinions or inferences upon the subject, the facts or data need not be admissible in evidence."

truth of the matter it asserted. The Supreme Court of Illinois also affirmed. Under state law, the court noted, the Cellmark report could not be used as substantive evidence. When Lambatos referenced the report during her direct examination, she did so "for the limited purpose of explaining the basis for [her expert opinion]," not for the purpose of showing "the truth of the matter asserted" by the report. Thus, the report was not used to establish its truth, but only "to show the underlying facts and data Lambatos used before rendering an expert opinion." We granted certiorari.

II A

The Confrontation Clause of the Sixth Amendment provides that in "all criminal prosecutions, the accused shall enjoy the right ... to be confronted with the witnesses against him." Before *Crawford,* this Court took the view that the Confrontation Clause did not bar the admission of an out-of-court statement that fell within a firmly rooted exception to the hearsay rule, see Ohio v. Roberts, 448 U.S. 56 (1980), but in *Crawford,* the Court adopted a fundamentally new interpretation of the confrontation right, holding that "testimonial statements of witnesses absent from trial [can be] admitted only where the declarant is unavailable, and only where the defendant has had a prior opportunity to cross-examine." *Crawford* has resulted in a steady stream of new cases in this Court.

Two [recent post-*Crawford*] decisions involved scientific reports. In Melendez–Diaz, 557 U.S. 305 (2009), the defendant was arrested and charged with distributing and trafficking in cocaine. At trial, the prosecution introduced bags of a white powdery substance that had been found in the defendant's possession. The trial court also admitted into evidence three "certificates of analysis" from the state forensic laboratory stating that the bags had been "examined with the following results: The substance was found to contain: Cocaine."

The Court held that the admission of these certificates, which were executed under oath before a notary, violated the Sixth Amendment. They were created for "the sole purpose of providing evidence against a defendant," and were "quite plainly affidavits." The Court emphasized that the introduction of the report to prove the nature of the substance found in the defendant's possession was tantamount to "live, in-court testimony" on that critical fact and that the certificates did "precisely what a witness does on direct examination." There was no doubt that the certificates were used to prove the truth of the matter they asserted. Under state law, "the sole purpose of the affidavits was to provide prima facie evidence of the composition, quality, and the net weight of the analyzed substance." On these facts, the Court said, it was clear that the certificates were "testimonial statements" that could not be introduced unless their authors were subjected to the "crucible of cross-examination."

In Bullcoming v. New Mexico, 564 U.S. ___ (2011), we held that another scientific report could not be used as substantive evidence against the defendant unless the analyst who prepared and certified the report was subject to confrontation. The defendant in that case had been convicted of driving while intoxicated. At trial, the court admitted into evidence a forensic report certifying that a sample of the defendant's blood had an alcohol concentration of 0.21 grams per hundred milliliters, well above the legal limit. Instead of calling the analyst who signed and certified the forensic report, the prosecution called another analyst who had not performed or observed the actual analysis, but was only familiar with the general testing procedures of the laboratory. The Court declined to accept this surrogate testimony, despite the fact that the testifying analyst was a "knowledgeable representative of the laboratory" who could "explain the lab's processes and the details of the report." The Court stated simply: "The accused's right is to be confronted with the analyst who made the certification."

Just as in *Melendez–Diaz,* the forensic report that was introduced in *Bullcoming* contained "a testimonial certification, made in order to prove a fact at a criminal trial." The report was signed by the nontestifying analyst who had authored it, stating, "I certify that I followed the procedures set out on the reverse of this report, and the statements in this block are correct. The concentration of alcohol in this sample is based on the grams of alcohol in one hundred milliliters of blood." Critically, the report was introduced at trial for the substantive purpose of proving the truth of the matter asserted by its out-of-court author—namely, that the defendant had a blood-alcohol level of 0.21. This was the central fact in question at the defendant's trial, and it was dispositive of his guilt.

In concurrence, Justice Sotomayor highlighted the importance of the fact that the forensic report had been admitted into evidence for the purpose of proving the truth of the matter it asserted. She emphasized that "this [was] not a case in which an expert witness was asked for his independent opinion about underlying testimonial reports that were not themselves admitted into evidence." We would face a different question, she observed, "if asked to determine the constitutionality of allowing an expert witness to discuss others' testimonial statements if the testimonial statements were not themselves admitted as evidence." We now confront that question.

B

It has long been accepted that an expert witness may voice an opinion based on facts concerning the events at issue in a particular case even if the expert lacks first-hand knowledge of those facts.

At common law, courts developed two ways to deal with this situation. An expert could rely on facts that had already been established in the record. But because it was not always possible to proceed in this manner, and because record evidence was often disputed, courts developed the alternative practice of allowing an expert to testify in the form of a "hypothetical question." Under this approach, the expert would be asked to assume the truth of certain factual predicates, and was then asked to offer an opinion based on those assumptions. The truth of the premises could then be established through independent evidence, and the factfinder would regard the expert's testimony to be only as credible as the premises on which it was based....

There is a long tradition of the use of hypothetical questions in American courts...

Modern rules of evidence continue to permit experts to express opinions based on facts about which they lack personal knowledge, but these rules dispense with the need for hypothetical questions. Under both the Illinois and the Federal Rules of Evidence, an expert may base an opinion on facts that are "made known to the expert at or before the hearing," but such reliance does not constitute admissible evidence of this underlying information. Ill. Rule Evid. 703; Fed. Rule Evid. 703. Accordingly, *in jury trials,* both Illinois and federal law generally bar an expert from disclosing such inadmissible evidence.[2] In bench trials, however, both the Illinois and the Federal Rules place no restriction on the revelation of such information to the factfinder. When the judge sits

---

[2] But disclosure of these facts or data to the jury is permitted if the value of disclosure "substantially outweighs [any] prejudicial effect," Fed. Rule Evid. 703, or "the probative value ... outweighs the risk of unfair prejudice." When this disclosure occurs, "the underlying facts" are revealed to the jury "for the limited purpose of explaining the basis for [the expert's] opinion" and not "for the truth of the matter asserted."

as the trier of fact, it is presumed that the judge will understand the limited reason for the disclosure of the underlying inadmissible information and will not rely on that information for any improper purpose. As we have noted, in bench trials, "judges routinely hear inadmissible evidence that they are presumed to ignore when making decisions." There is a well-established presumption that *"the judge [has] adhered to basic rules of procedure,"* when the judge is acting as a factfinder.

This feature of Illinois and federal law is important because *Crawford,* while departing from prior Confrontation Clause precedent in other respects, took pains to reaffirm the proposition that the Confrontation Clause "does not bar the use of testimonial statements for purposes other than establishing the truth of the matter asserted."...

III

In order to assess petitioner's Confrontation Clause argument, it is helpful to inventory exactly what Lambatos said on the stand about Cellmark. She testified to the truth of the following matters: Cellmark was an accredited lab; the ISP occasionally sent forensic samples to Cellmark for DNA testing; according to shipping manifests admitted into evidence, the ISP lab sent vaginal swabs taken from the victim to Cellmark and later received those swabs back from Cellmark; and, finally, the Cellmark DNA profile matched a profile produced by the ISP lab from a sample of petitioner's blood. Lambatos had personal knowledge of all of these matters, and therefore none of this testimony infringed petitioner's confrontation right.

Lambatos did not testify to the truth of any other matter concerning Cellmark. She made no other reference to the Cellmark report, which was not admitted into evidence and was not seen by the trier of fact. Nor did she testify to anything that was done at the Cellmark lab, and she did not vouch for the quality of Cellmark's work.

The principal argument advanced to show a Confrontation Clause violation concerns the phrase that Lambatos used when she referred to the DNA profile that the ISP lab received from Cellmark...

In the view of the dissent, the following is the critical portion of Lambatos' testimony, with the particular words that the dissent finds objectionable italicized:

Q. Was there a computer match generated of the male DNA profile *found in semen from the vaginal swabs of [L.J.]* to a male DNA

profile that had been identified as having originated from Sandy Williams?
A. Yes, there was.

According to the dissent, the italicized phrase violated petitioner's confrontation right because Lambatos lacked personal knowledge that the profile produced by Cellmark was based on the vaginal swabs taken from the victim, L.J. As the dissent acknowledges, there would have been "nothing wrong with Lambatos's testifying that two DNA profiles—the one shown in the Cellmark report and the one derived from Williams's blood—matched each other; that was a straightforward application of Lambatos's expertise." Thus, if Lambatos' testimony had been slightly modified as follows, the dissent would see no problem:

> Q. Was there a computer match generated of the male DNA profile *produced by Cellmark* to a male DNA profile that had been identified as having originated from Sandy Williams?
> A. Yes, there was.

The defect in this argument is that under Illinois law (like federal law) it is clear that the putatively offending phrase in Lambatos' testimony was not admissible for the purpose of proving the truth of the matter asserted—*i.e.,* that the matching DNA profile was "found in semen from the vaginal swabs." Rather, that fact was a mere premise of the prosecutor's question, and Lambatos simply assumed that premise to be true when she gave her answer indicating that there was a match between the two DNA profiles. There is no reason to think that the trier of fact took Lambatos' answer as substantive evidence to establish where the DNA profiles came from.

The dissent's argument would have force if petitioner had elected to have a jury trial. In that event, there would have been a danger of the jury's taking Lambatos' testimony as proof that the Cellmark profile was derived from the sample obtained from the victim's vaginal swabs. Absent an evaluation of the risk of juror confusion and careful jury instructions, the testimony could not have gone to the jury.

This case, however, involves *a bench trial* and we must assume that the trial judge understood that the portion of Lambatos' testimony to which the dissent objects was not admissible to prove the truth of the matter asserted. The dissent, on the other hand, reaches the truly remarkable conclusion that the wording of Lambatos' testimony

136

confused the trial judge. Were it not for that wording, the argument goes, the judge might have found that the prosecution failed to introduce sufficient admissible evidence to show that the Cellmark profile was derived from the sample taken from the victim, and the judge might have disregarded the DNA evidence. This argument reflects a profound lack of respect for the acumen of the trial judge....

To begin, the dissent's argument finds no support in the trial record.... Second, it is extraordinarily unlikely that any trial judge would be confused in the way that the dissent posits.... Third, the admissible evidence left little room for argument that the sample tested by Cellmark came from any source other than the victim's vaginal swabs. This is so because there is simply no plausible explanation for how Cellmark could have produced a DNA profile that matched Williams' if Cellmark had tested any sample other than the one taken from the victim. If any other items that might have contained Williams' DNA had been sent to Cellmark or were otherwise in Cellmark's possession, there would have been a chance of a mix-up or of cross-contamination. But there is absolutely nothing to suggest that Cellmark had any such items. Thus, the fact that the Cellmark profile matched Williams—the very man whom the victim identified in a lineup and at trial as her attacker—was itself striking confirmation that the sample that Cellmark tested was the sample taken from the victim's vaginal swabs. For these reasons, it is fanciful to suggest that the trial judge took Lambatos' testimony as providing critical chain-of-custody evidence.

[Even] if the record did not contain any evidence that could rationally support a finding that Cellmark produced a scientifically reliable DNA profile based on L.J.'s vaginal swab, that would not establish a Confrontation Clause violation. If there were no proof that Cellmark produced an accurate profile based on that sample, Lambatos' testimony regarding the match would be irrelevant, but the Confrontation Clause, as interpreted in *Crawford,* does not bar the admission of irrelevant evidence, only testimonial statements by declarants who are not subject to cross-examination....

This conclusion is entirely consistent with *Bullcoming* and *Melendez–Diaz.* In those cases, the forensic reports were introduced into evidence, and there is no question that this was done for the purpose of proving the truth of what they asserted: in *Bullcoming* that the defendant's blood alcohol level exceeded the legal limit and in *Melendez–Diaz* that the substance in question contained cocaine.

Nothing comparable happened here. In this case, the Cellmark report was not introduced into evidence. An expert witness referred to the report not to prove the truth of the matter asserted in the report, *i.e.,* that the report contained an accurate profile of the perpetrator's DNA, but only to establish that the report contained a DNA profile that matched the DNA profile deduced from petitioner's blood....

IV

Even if the Cellmark report had been introduced for its truth, we would nevertheless conclude that there was no Confrontation Clause violation. The Confrontation Clause refers to testimony by "witnesses against" an accused. Both the noted evidence scholar James Henry Wigmore and Justice Harlan interpreted the Clause in a strictly literal sense as referring solely to persons who testify in court, but we have not adopted this narrow view. It has been said that the "difficulty with the Wigmore–Harlan view in its purest form is its tension with much of the apparent history surrounding the evolution of the right of confrontation at common law." The "principal evil at which the Confrontation Clause was directed," the Court concluded in *Crawford,* "was the civil-law mode of criminal procedure, and particularly its use of *ex parte* examinations as evidence against the accused." In England, "pretrial examinations of suspects and witnesses by government officials were sometimes read in court in lieu of live testimony." The Court has thus interpreted the Confrontation Clause as prohibiting modern-day practices that are tantamount to the abuses that gave rise to the recognition of the confrontation right. But any further expansion would strain the constitutional text.

The abuses that the Court has identified as prompting the adoption of the Confrontation Clause shared the following two characteristics: (a) they involved out-of-court statements having the primary purpose of accusing a targeted individual of engaging in criminal conduct and (b) they involved formalized statements such as affidavits, depositions, prior testimony, or confessions....

In *Melendez–Diaz* and *Bullcoming,* the Court held that the particular forensic reports at issue qualified as testimonial statements, but the Court did not hold that all forensic reports fall into the same category. Introduction of the reports in those cases ran afoul of the Confrontation Clause because they were the equivalent of affidavits made for the purpose of proving the guilt of a particular criminal defendant at trial.

There was nothing resembling an ongoing emergency, as the suspects in both cases had already been captured, and the tests in question were relatively simple and can generally be performed by a single analyst. In addition, the technicians who prepared the reports must have realized that their contents (which reported an elevated blood-alcohol level and the presence of an illegal drug) would be incriminating.

The Cellmark report is very different. It plainly was not prepared for the primary purpose of accusing a targeted individual. In identifying the primary purpose of an out-of-court statement, we apply an objective test. We look for the primary purpose that a reasonable person would have ascribed to the statement, taking into account all of the surrounding circumstances.

Here, the primary purpose of the Cellmark report, viewed objectively, was not to accuse petitioner or to create evidence for use at trial. When the ISP lab sent the sample to Cellmark, its primary purpose was to catch a dangerous rapist who was still at large, not to obtain evidence for use against petitioner, who was neither in custody nor under suspicion at that time. Similarly, no one at Cellmark could have possibly known that the profile that it produced would turn out to inculpate petitioner—or for that matter, anyone else whose DNA profile was in a law enforcement database. Under these circumstances, there was no "prospect of fabrication" and no incentive to produce anything other than a scientifically sound and reliable profile.

The situation in which the Cellmark technicians found themselves was by no means unique. When lab technicians are asked to work on the production of a DNA profile, they often have no idea what the consequences of their work will be. In some cases, a DNA profile may provide powerful incriminating evidence against a person who is identified either before or after the profile is completed. But in others, the primary effect of the profile is to exonerate a suspect who has been charged or is under investigation. The technicians who prepare a DNA profile generally have no way of knowing whether it will turn out to be incriminating or exonerating—or both.

It is also significant that in many labs, numerous technicians work on each DNA profile. When the work of a lab is divided up in such a way, it is likely that the sole purpose of each technician is simply to perform his or her task in accordance with accepted procedures.

Finally, the knowledge that defects in a DNA profile may often be detected from the profile itself provides a further safeguard.... At the time of the testing, petitioner had not yet been identified as a suspect, and there is no suggestion that anyone at Cellmark had a sample of his DNA to swap in by malice or mistake. And given the complexity of the DNA molecule, it is inconceivable that shoddy lab work would somehow produce a DNA profile that just so happened to have the precise genetic makeup of petitioner, who just so happened to be picked out of a lineup by the victim. The prospect is beyond fanciful.

In short, the use at trial of a DNA report prepared by a modern, accredited laboratory "bears little if any resemblance to the historical practices that the Confrontation Clause aimed to eliminate."

For the two independent reasons explained above, we conclude that there was no Confrontation Clause violation in this case....

BREYER, J., concurring.

This case raises a question that I believe neither the plurality nor the dissent answers adequately: How does the Confrontation Clause apply to the panoply of crime laboratory reports and underlying technical statements written by (or otherwise made by) laboratory technicians? In this context, what, if any, are the outer limits of the "testimonial statements" rule set forth in Crawford v. Washington? Because I believe the question difficult, important, and not squarely addressed either today or in our earlier opinions, and because I believe additional briefing would help us find a proper, generally applicable answer, I would set this case for re-argument. In the absence of doing so, I adhere to the dissenting views set forth in Melendez–Diaz v. Massachusetts and Bullcoming v. New Mexico. I also join the plurality's opinion.

This case is another in our series involving the intersection of the Confrontation Clause and expert testimony.... The Confrontation Clause problem lies in the fact that Lambatos did not have personal knowledge that the male DNA profile that Cellmark said was derived from the crime victim's vaginal swab sample was in fact correctly derived from that sample. And no Cellmark expert testified that it was true. Rather, she simply relied for her knowledge of the fact upon Cellmark's report. And the defendant Williams had no opportunity to cross-examine the individual or individuals who produced that report.

[The] plurality explains why it finds that admission of Lambatos' testimony nonetheless did not violate the Confrontation Clause.... Under well-established principles of evidence, experts may rely on otherwise inadmissible out-of-court statements as a basis for forming an expert opinion if they are of a kind that experts in the field normally rely upon. Nor need the prosecution enter those out-of-court statements into evidence for their truth. That, the Illinois courts held, is just what took place here.

The dissent would abandon this well-established rule. It would not permit Lambatos to offer an expert opinion in reliance on the Cellmark report unless the prosecution also produces one or more experts who wrote or otherwise produced the report. I am willing to accept the dissent's characterization of the present rule as artificial, but I am not certain that the dissent has produced a workable alternative.

Once one abandons the traditional rule, there would seem often to be no logical stopping place between requiring the prosecution to call as a witness one of the laboratory experts who worked on the matter and requiring the prosecution to call *all* of the laboratory experts who did so. Experts—especially laboratory experts—regularly rely on the technical statements and results of other experts to form their own opinions. The reality of the matter is that the introduction of a laboratory report involves layer upon layer of technical statements (express or implied) made by one expert and relied upon by another. Hence my general question: How does the Confrontation Clause apply to crime laboratory reports and underlying technical statements made by laboratory technicians? ...

In the absence of re-argument, I adhere to the dissenting view set forth in *Melendez–Diaz* and *Bullcoming,* under which the Cellmark report would not be considered "testimonial" and barred by the Confrontation Clause. That view understands the Confrontation Clause as interpreted in *Crawford* to bar the admission of *testimonial* statements made out of court unless the declarant is unavailable and the defendant had a prior opportunity to cross-examine. It also understands the word "testimonial" as having outer limits and *Crawford* as describing a constitutional heartland. And that view would leave the States with constitutional leeway to maintain traditional expert testimony rules as well as hearsay exceptions where there are strong reasons for doing so and *Crawford*'s basic rationale does not apply.

In particular, the States could create an exception that presumptively would allow introduction of DNA reports from accredited crime laboratories. The defendant would remain free to call laboratory technicians as witnesses. Were there significant reason to question a laboratory's technical competence or its neutrality, the presumptive exception would disappear, thereby requiring the prosecution to produce any relevant technical witnesses. Such an exception would lie outside *Crawford*'s constitutional limits.

[To] bar admission of the out-of-court records at issue here could undermine, not fortify, the accuracy of factfinding at a criminal trial. Such a precedent could bar the admission of other reliable case-specific technical information such as, say, autopsy reports. Autopsies, like the DNA report in this case, are often conducted when it is not yet clear whether there is a particular suspect or whether the facts found in the autopsy will ultimately prove relevant in a criminal trial. Autopsies are typically conducted soon after death. And when, say, a victim's body has decomposed, repetition of the autopsy may not be possible. What is to happen if the medical examiner dies before trial? Is the Confrontation Clause effectively to function as a statute of limitations for murder? ...

Consequently, I would consider reports such as the DNA report before us presumptively to lie outside the perimeter of the Clause as established by the Court's precedents. Such a holding leaves the defendant free to call the laboratory employee as a witness if the employee is available. Moreover, should the defendant provide good reason to doubt the laboratory's competence or the validity of its accreditation, then the alternative safeguard of reliability would no longer exist and the Constitution would entitle defendant to Confrontation Clause protection. Similarly, should the defendant demonstrate the existence of a motive to falsify, then the alternative safeguard of honesty would no longer exist and the Constitution would entitle the defendant to Confrontation Clause protection. Thus, the defendant would remain free to show the absence or inadequacy of the alternative reliability/honesty safeguards, thereby rebutting the presumption and making the Confrontation Clause applicable. No one has suggested any such problem in respect to the Cellmark Report at issue here....

Because the plurality's opinion is basically consistent with the views set forth here, I join that opinion in full.

THOMAS, J., concurring in the judgment.

I agree with the plurality that the disclosure of Cellmark's out-of-court statements through the expert testimony of Sandra Lambatos did not violate the Confrontation Clause. I reach this conclusion, however, solely because Cellmark's statements lacked the requisite "formality and solemnity" to be considered "testimonial" for purposes of the Confrontation Clause. As I explain below, I share the dissent's view of the plurality's flawed analysis.

I

The threshold question in this case is whether Cellmark's statements were hearsay at all. As the Court has explained, the Confrontation Clause "does not bar the use of testimonial statements for purposes other than establishing the truth of the matter asserted." Here, the State of Illinois contends that Cellmark's statements—that it successfully derived a male DNA profile and that the profile came from L.J.'s swabs—were introduced only to show the basis of Lambatos' opinion, and not for their truth. In my view, however, there was no plausible reason for the introduction of Cellmark's statements other than to establish their truth.

Illinois Rule of Evidence 703 and its federal counterpart permit an expert to base his opinion on facts about which he lacks personal knowledge and to disclose those facts to the trier of fact. Relying on these Rules, the State contends that the facts on which an expert's opinion relies are not to be considered for their truth, but only to explain the basis of his opinion. Accordingly, in the State's view, the disclosure of expert "basis testimony" does not implicate the Confrontation Clause.

I do not think that rules of evidence should so easily trump a defendant's confrontation right. To be sure, we should not "lightly [sweep] away an accepted rule" of federal or state evidence law when applying the Confrontation Clause. Rules of limited admissibility are commonplace in evidence law. And, we often presume that courts and juries follow limiting instructions. But we have recognized that concepts central to the application of the Confrontation Clause are ultimately matters of federal constitutional law that are not dictated by state or federal evidentiary rules. Likewise, we have held that limiting instructions may be insufficient in some circumstances to protect against violations of the Confrontation Clause. See Bruton v. United States, 391 U.S. 123 (1968).

Of particular importance here, we have made sure that an out-of-court statement was introduced for a "*legitimate,* nonhearsay purpose" before relying on the not-for-its-truth rationale to dismiss the application of the Confrontation Clause.

[Statements] introduced to explain the basis of an expert's opinion are not introduced for a plausible nonhearsay purpose. There is no meaningful distinction between disclosing an out-of-court statement so that the factfinder may evaluate the expert's opinion and disclosing that statement for its truth. "To use the inadmissible information in evaluating the expert's testimony, the jury must make a preliminary judgment about whether this information is true." D. Kaye, D. Bernstein, & J. Mnookin, The New Wigmore: A Treatise on Evidence: Expert Evidence § 4.10.1, p. 196 (2d ed. 2011) (hereinafter Kaye). "If the jury believes that the basis evidence is true, it will likely also believe that the expert's reliance is justified; inversely, if the jury doubts the accuracy or validity of the basis evidence, it will be skeptical of the expert's conclusions."[1]

Contrary to the plurality's suggestion, this commonsense conclusion is not undermined by any longstanding historical practice exempting expert basis testimony from the rigors of the Confrontation Clause...

Those concerns are fully applicable in this case. Lambatos opined that petitioner's DNA profile matched the male profile derived from L.J.'s vaginal swabs. In reaching that conclusion, Lambatos relied on Cellmark's out-of-court statements that the profile it reported was in fact derived from L.J.'s swabs, rather than from some other source. Thus, the validity of Lambatos' opinion ultimately turned on the truth of Cellmark's statements. The plurality's assertion that Cellmark's statements were merely relayed to explain the assumptions on which Lambatos' opinion rested overlooks that the value of Lambatos' testimony depended on the truth of those very assumptions....

The plurality's contrary conclusion may seem of little consequence to those who view DNA testing and other forms of "hard science" as intrinsically reliable. Today's holding, however, will reach beyond scientific evidence to ordinary out-of-court statements. For example, it is not uncommon for experts to rely on interviews with third parties in forming their opinions. It is no answer to say that "safeguards" in the rules of evidence will prevent the abuse of basis testimony....

II

---

[1] The plurality relies heavily on the fact that this case involved a bench trial, emphasizing that a judge sitting as factfinder is presumed—more so than a jury—to "understand the limited reason for the disclosure" of basis testimony and to "not rely on that information for any improper purpose." Even accepting that presumption, the point is not that the factfinder is unable to understand the restricted purpose for basis testimony. Instead, the point is that the purportedly "limited reason" for such testimony—to aid the factfinder in evaluating the expert's opinion—necessarily entails an evaluation of whether the basis testimony is true.

Having concluded that the statements at issue here were introduced for their truth, I turn to whether they were "testimonial" for purposes of the Confrontation Clause. In *Crawford,* the Court explained that the "text of the Confrontation Clause ... applies to 'witnesses' against the accused—in other words, those who bear testimony." Testimony, in turn, is a "solemn declaration or affirmation made for the purpose of establishing or proving some fact." In light of its text, I continue to think that the Confrontation Clause regulates only the use of statements bearing "indicia of solemnity." Davis v. Washington, 547 U.S. 813 (2006) (Thomas, J., concurring in judgment in part and dissenting in part). This test comports with history because solemnity marked the practices that the Confrontation Clause was designed to eliminate, namely, the *ex parte* examination of witnesses under the English bail and committal statutes passed during the reign of Queen Mary. Accordingly, I have concluded that the Confrontation Clause reaches formalized testimonial materials, such as depositions, affidavits, and prior testimony, or statements resulting from "formalized dialogue," such as custodial interrogation.[5]

Applying these principles, I conclude that Cellmark's report is not a statement by a "witness" within the meaning of the Confrontation Clause. The Cellmark report lacks the solemnity of an affidavit or deposition, for it is neither a sworn nor a certified declaration of fact. Nowhere does the report attest that its statements accurately reflect the DNA testing processes used or the results obtained. The report is signed by two "reviewers," but they neither purport to have performed the DNA testing nor certify the accuracy of those who did. And, although the report was produced at the request of law enforcement, it was not the product of any sort of formalized dialogue resembling custodial interrogation.

The Cellmark report is distinguishable from the laboratory reports that we determined were testimonial in *Melendez–Diaz,* and in Bullcoming v. New Mexico. In *Melendez–Diaz,* the reports in question were sworn to before a notary public by the analysts who tested a substance for cocaine. In *Bullcoming,* the report, though unsworn,

---

[5] In addition, I have stated that, because the Confrontation Clause "sought to regulate prosecutorial abuse occurring through use of *ex parte* statements," it "also reaches the use of technically informal statements when used to evade the formalized process." But, in this case, there is no indication that Cellmark's statements were offered "in order to evade confrontation."

included a "Certificate of Analyst" signed by the forensic analyst who tested the defendant's blood sample. The analyst affirmed that the seal of the sample was received intact and broken in the laboratory, that the statements in the analyst's block of the report are correct, and that he had followed the procedures set out on the reverse of the report.

The dissent insists that the *Bullcoming* report and Cellmark's report are equally formal, separated only by such "minutia" as the fact that Cellmark's report is not labeled a "certificate." To the contrary, what distinguishes the two is that Cellmark's report, in substance, certifies nothing. That distinction is constitutionally significant because the scope of the confrontation right is properly limited to extrajudicial statements similar in solemnity to the Marian examination practices that the Confrontation Clause was designed to prevent. By certifying the truth of the analyst's representations, the unsworn *Bullcoming* report bore a striking resemblance to the Marian practice in which magistrates examined witnesses, typically on oath, and certified the results to the court. And, in *Melendez–Diaz,* we observed that "certificates are functionally identical to live, in-court testimony, doing precisely what a witness does on direct examination." Cellmark's report is marked by no such indicia of solemnity....

Respondent and its *amici* have emphasized the economic and logistical burdens that would be visited upon States should every analyst who reports DNA results be required to testify at trial. These burdens are largely the product of a primary purpose test that reaches out-of-court statements well beyond the historical scope of the Confrontation Clause and thus sweeps in a broad range of sources on which modern experts regularly rely. The proper solution to this problem is not to carve out a Confrontation Clause exception for expert testimony that is rooted only in legal fiction. Nor is it to create a new primary purpose test that ensures that DNA evidence is treated differently. Rather, the solution is to adopt a reading of the Confrontation Clause that respects its historically limited application to a narrow class of statements bearing indicia of solemnity. In forgoing that approach, today's decision diminishes the Confrontation Clause's protection in cases where experts convey the contents of solemn, formalized statements to explain the bases for their opinions. These are the very cases in which the accused *should* "enjoy the right ... to be confronted with the witnesses against him."

KAGAN, J., dissenting.[*]

... In two decisions issued in the last three years, this Court held that if a prosecutor wants to introduce the results of forensic testing into evidence, he must afford the defendant an opportunity to cross-examine an analyst responsible for the test. Forensic evidence is reliable only when properly produced, and the Confrontation Clause prescribes a particular method for determining whether that has happened.... Hence the genius of an 18th-century device as applied to 21st-century evidence: Cross-examination of the analyst is especially likely to reveal whether vials have been switched, samples contaminated, tests incompetently run, or results inaccurately recorded.

Under our Confrontation Clause precedents, this is an open-and-shut case. The State of Illinois prosecuted Sandy Williams for rape based in part on a DNA profile created in Cellmark's laboratory. Yet the State did not give Williams a chance to question the analyst who produced that evidence. Instead, the prosecution introduced the results of Cellmark's testing through an expert witness who had no idea how they were generated. That approach—no less (perhaps more) than the confrontation-free methods of presenting forensic evidence we have formerly banned—deprived Williams of his Sixth Amendment right to confront the witnesses against him.

The Court today disagrees, though it cannot settle on a reason why.... Because defendants like Williams have a constitutional right to confront the witnesses against them, I respectfully dissent from the Court's fractured decision.

I

... The report at issue here shows a DNA profile produced by an analyst at Cellmark's laboratory, allegedly from a vaginal swab taken from a young woman, L.J., after she was raped. That report is identical to the one in *Bullcoming* (and *Melendez–Diaz*) in all material respects. Once again, the report was made to establish some fact in a criminal proceeding—here, the identity of L.J.'s attacker. And once again, it details the results of forensic testing on evidence gathered by the police. Viewed side-by-side with the *Bullcoming* report, the Cellmark analysis has a comparable title; similarly describes the relevant samples, test methodology, and results; and likewise includes the signatures of

---

[*] [Justices Scalia, Ginsburg and Sotomayor joined this dissent. —EDS.]

laboratory officials. So under this Court's prior analysis, the substance of the report could come into evidence only if Williams had a chance to cross-examine the responsible analyst.

But that is not what happened. Instead, the prosecutor used Sandra Lambatos—a state-employed scientist who had not participated in the testing—as the conduit for this piece of evidence. Lambatos came to the stand after two other state analysts testified about forensic tests they had performed. One recounted how she had developed a DNA profile of Sandy Williams from a blood sample drawn after his arrest. And another told how he had confirmed the presence of (unidentified) semen on the vaginal swabs taken from L.J. All this was by the book: Williams had an opportunity to cross-examine both witnesses about the tests they had run. But of course, the State still needed to supply the missing link—it had to show that DNA found in the semen on L.J.'s vaginal swabs matched Williams's DNA. To fill that gap, the prosecutor could have called the analyst from Cellmark to testify about the DNA profile she had produced from the swabs. But instead, the State called Lambatos as an expert witness and had her testify that the semen on those swabs contained Sandy Williams's DNA:

> Q. Was there a computer match generated of the male DNA profile found in semen from the vaginal swabs of [L.J.] to a male DNA profile that had been identified as having originated from Sandy Williams?
> A. Yes, there was.
> Q. Did you compare the semen ... from the vaginal swabs of [L.J.] to the male DNA profile ... from the blood of Sandy Williams?
> A. Yes, I did. ...
> Q. [Is] the semen identified in the vaginal swabs of [L.J.] consistent with having originated from Sandy Williams?
> A. Yes.

And so it was Lambatos, rather than any Cellmark employee, who informed the trier of fact that the testing of L.J.'s vaginal swabs had produced a male DNA profile implicating Williams....

Lambatos's testimony is functionally identical to the "surrogate testimony" that New Mexico proffered in *Bullcoming,* which did nothing to cure the problem identified in *Melendez–Diaz* (which, for its part, straightforwardly applied our decision in *Crawford*). Like the surrogate witness in *Bullcoming,* Lambatos "could not convey what [the actual analyst] knew or observed about the events ... , *i.e.,* the particular test and testing process he employed." Nor could such surrogate testimony expose any lapses or lies on the testing analyst's part. Like the lawyers in *Melendez–Diaz* and *Bullcoming,* Williams's attorney could not ask questions about that analyst's "proficiency, the care he took in performing his work, and his veracity." He could not probe whether the analyst had tested the wrong vial, inverted the labels on the samples, committed some more technical error, or simply made up the results. Indeed, Williams's lawyer was even more hamstrung than Bullcoming's. At least the surrogate witness in *Bullcoming* worked at the relevant laboratory and was familiar with its procedures. That is not true of Lambatos: She had no knowledge at all of Cellmark's operations. Indeed, for all the record discloses, she may never have set foot in Cellmark's laboratory.

Under our case law, that is sufficient to resolve this case. When the State elected to introduce the substance of Cellmark's report into evidence, the analyst who generated that report became a witness whom Williams had the right to confront....

II

... The plurality tries to make plausible its not-for-the-truth rationale by rewriting Lambatos's testimony about the Cellmark report. According to the plurality, Lambatos merely "assumed" that Cellmark's DNA profile came from L.J.'s vaginal swabs, accepting for the sake of argument the prosecutor's premise. But that is incorrect. Nothing in Lambatos's testimony indicates that she was making an assumption or considering a hypothesis. To the contrary, Lambatos affirmed, without qualification, that the Cellmark report showed a "male DNA profile found in semen from the vaginal swabs of [L.J.]." Had she done otherwise, this case would be different. There was nothing wrong with Lambatos's testifying that two DNA profiles—the one shown in the Cellmark report and the one derived from Williams's blood—matched each other; that was a straightforward application of Lambatos's expertise. Similarly, Lambatos could have added that *if* the Cellmark report resulted from scientifically sound testing of L.J.'s vaginal swab, *then* it would link Williams to the assault. What Lambatos could not do was what she did: indicate that the Cellmark report *was* produced in this way by saying that L.J.'s vaginal swab contained DNA matching Williams's. By testifying in that manner, Lambatos became just like the surrogate witness in *Bullcoming*—a person knowing nothing about the particular test and testing process, but vouching for them regardless. We have held that the Confrontation Clause requires something more....

Imagine for a moment a poorly trained, incompetent, or dishonest laboratory analyst. (The analyst in *Bullcoming,* placed on unpaid leave for unknown reasons, might qualify.) Under our precedents, the prosecutor cannot avoid exposing that analyst to cross-examination simply by introducing his report. Nor can the prosecutor escape that fate by offering the results through the testimony of another analyst from the laboratory. But under the plurality's approach, the prosecutor could choose the analyst-witness of his dreams (as the judge here said, "the best DNA witness I have ever heard"), offer her as an expert (she knows nothing about the test, but boasts impressive degrees), and have her provide testimony identical to the best the actual tester might have given ("the DNA extracted from the vaginal swabs matched Sandy Williams's")—all so long as a state evidence rule says that the purpose of the testimony is to enable the factfinder to assess the expert opinion's basis.... If the Confrontation Clause prevents the State from getting its evidence in through the front door, then the State could sneak it in through the back. What a neat trick—but really, what a way to run a criminal justice system. No wonder five Justices reject it....

Before today's decision, a prosecutor wishing to admit the results of forensic testing had to produce the technician responsible for the analysis. That was the result of not one, but two decisions this Court issued in the last three years. But that clear rule is clear no longer. The five Justices who control the outcome of today's case agree on very little. Among them, though, they can boast of two accomplishments. First, they have approved the introduction of testimony at Williams's trial that the Confrontation Clause, rightly understood, clearly prohibits. Second, they have left significant confusion in their wake. What comes out of four Justices' desire to limit *Melendez–Diaz* and *Bullcoming* in whatever way possible, combined with one Justice's one-justice view of those holdings, is—to be frank—who knows what....

The better course in this case would have been simply to follow *Melendez–Diaz* and *Bullcoming*.... And until a majority of this Court reverses or confines those decisions, I would understand them as continuing to govern, in every particular, the admission of forensic evidence....

Michigan v. Richard Perry Bryant
131 S. Ct. 1142 (2011)

SOTOMAYOR, J.[*]

At respondent Richard Bryant's trial, the court admitted statements that the victim, Anthony Covington, made to police officers who discovered him mortally wounded in a gas station parking lot. A jury convicted Bryant of, *inter alia,* second-degree murder.... We hold that the circumstances of the interaction between Covington and the police objectively indicate that the primary purpose of the interrogation was "to enable police assistance to meet an ongoing emergency." Therefore, Covington's identification and description of the shooter and the location of the shooting were not testimonial statements, and their admission at Bryant's trial did not violate the Confrontation Clause....

I

Around 3:25 A.M. on April 29, 2001, Detroit, Michigan police officers responded to a radio dispatch indicating that a man had been shot. At the scene, they found the victim, Anthony Covington, lying on the ground next to his car in a gas station parking lot. Covington had a gunshot wound to his abdomen, appeared to be in great pain, and spoke with difficulty.

The police asked him what had happened, who had shot him, and where the shooting had occurred. Covington stated that "Rick" shot him at around 3 A.M. He also indicated that he had a conversation with Bryant, whom he recognized based on his voice, through the back door of Bryant's house. Covington explained that when he turned to leave, he was shot through the door and then drove to the gas station, where police found him.

Covington's conversation with the police ended within 5 to 10 minutes when emergency medical services arrived. Covington was transported to a hospital and died within hours. The police left the gas station after speaking with Covington, called for backup, and traveled to Bryant's house. They did not find Bryant there but did find blood and a bullet on the back porch and an apparent bullet hole in the back door. Police also found Covington's wallet and identification outside the house.

---

[*] Chief Justice Roberts and Justices Kennedy, Breyer, and Alito joined this opinion.

151

At trial, which occurred prior to our decisions in *Crawford* and *Davis,* the police officers who spoke with Covington at the gas station testified about what Covington had told them. The jury returned a guilty verdict on charges of second-degree murder, being a felon in possession of a firearm, and possession of a firearm during the commission of a felony. Bryant appealed, and the [Supreme Court of Michigan] reversed his conviction. ...

II

The Confrontation Clause of the Sixth Amendment states: "In all criminal prosecutions, the accused shall enjoy the right ... to be confronted with the witnesses against him." ... In Ohio v. Roberts, 448 U.S. 56 (1980), we explained that the confrontation right does not bar admission of statements of an unavailable witness if the statements bear adequate "indicia of reliability." We held that reliability can be established if "the evidence falls within a firmly rooted hearsay exception," or if it does not fall within such an exception, then if it bears "particularized guarantees of trustworthiness."

Nearly a quarter century later, we decided Crawford v. Washington, 541 U.S. 36 (2004). Petitioner Michael Crawford was prosecuted for stabbing a man who had allegedly attempted to rape his wife, Sylvia. Sylvia witnessed the stabbing, and later that night, after she and her husband were both arrested, police interrogated her about the incident. At trial, Sylvia Crawford claimed spousal privilege and did not testify, but the State introduced a tape recording of Sylvia's statement to the police in an effort to prove that the stabbing was not in self-defense, as Michael Crawford claimed. The Washington Supreme Court affirmed Crawford's conviction because it found Sylvia's statement to be reliable, as required under Ohio v. Roberts. We reversed, overruling Ohio v. Roberts.

Crawford examined the common-law history of the confrontation right and explained that "the principal evil at which the Confrontation Clause was directed was the civil-law mode of criminal procedure, and particularly its use of *ex parte* examinations as evidence against the accused." We noted that in England, pretrial examinations of suspects and witnesses by government officials "were sometimes read in court in lieu of live testimony." In light of this history, we emphasized the word "witnesses" in the Sixth Amendment, defining it as those who "bear testimony." We defined "testimony" as a "solemn declaration or affirmation made for the purpose of establishing or proving some fact."

We noted that an accuser who makes a formal statement to government officers "bears testimony in a sense that a person who makes a casual remark to an acquaintance does not." We therefore limited the Confrontation Clause's reach to testimonial statements and held that in order for testimonial evidence to be admissible, the Sixth Amendment "demands what the common law required: unavailability and a prior opportunity for cross-examination." Although leaving for another day any effort to spell out a comprehensive definition of "testimonial," *Crawford* noted that "at a minimum" it includes "prior testimony at a preliminary hearing, before a grand jury, or at a former trial; and ... police interrogations." ...

In 2006, the Court in Davis v. Washington and Hammon v. Indiana took a further step to determine more precisely which police interrogations produce testimony and therefore implicate a Confrontation Clause bar. ... *Davis* and *Hammon* were both domestic violence cases. In *Davis,* Michelle McCottry made the statements at issue to a 911 operator during a domestic disturbance with Adrian Davis, her former boyfriend. McCottry told the operator, "He's here jumpin' on me again," and, "He's usin' his fists." The operator then asked McCottry for Davis' first and last names and middle initial, and at that point in the conversation McCottry reported that Davis had fled in a car. McCottry did not appear at Davis' trial, and the State introduced the recording of her conversation with the 911 operator.

In *Hammon,* decided along with *Davis,* police responded to a domestic disturbance call at the home of Amy and Hershel Hammon, where they found Amy alone on the front porch. She appeared "somewhat frightened," but told them "nothing was the matter." She gave the police permission to enter the house, where they saw a gas heating unit with the glass front shattered on the floor. One officer remained in the kitchen with Hershel, while another officer talked to Amy in the living room about what had happened. Hershel tried several times to participate in Amy's conversation with the police and became angry when the police required him to stay separated from Amy. The police asked Amy to fill out and sign a battery affidavit. She wrote: "Broke our Furnace & shoved me down on the floor into the broken glass. Hit me in the chest and threw me down. Broke our lamps & phone. Tore up my van where I couldn't leave the house. Attacked my daughter." Amy did not appear at Hershel's trial, so the police officers who spoke with her testified as to her statements and authenticated the affidavit. ...

To address the facts of both cases, we expanded upon the meaning of "testimonial" that we first employed in *Crawford* and discussed the concept of an ongoing emergency. We explained:

> Statements are nontestimonial when made in the course of police interrogation under circumstances objectively indicating that the primary purpose of the interrogation is to enable police assistance to meet an ongoing emergency. They are testimonial when the circumstances objectively indicate that there is no such ongoing emergency, and that the primary purpose of the interrogation is to establish or prove past events potentially relevant to later criminal prosecution.

Examining the *Davis* and *Hammon* statements in light of those definitions, we held that the statements at issue in *Davis* were nontestimonial and the statements in *Hammon* were testimonial. We distinguished the statements in *Davis* from the testimonial statements in *Crawford* on several grounds, including that the victim in *Davis* was speaking about events *as they were actually happening,* rather than describing past events, that there was an ongoing emergency, that the elicited statements were necessary to be able to *resolve* the present emergency, and that the statements were not formal. In *Hammon,* on the other hand, we held that, "it is entirely clear from the circumstances that the interrogation was part of an investigation into possibly criminal past conduct." There was no emergency in progress. The officer questioning Amy "was not seeking to determine 'what is happening,' but rather 'what happened.'" It was "formal enough" that the police interrogated Amy in a room separate from her husband where, "some time after the events described were over," she "deliberately recounted, in response to police questioning, how potentially criminal past events began and progressed." Because her statements "were neither a cry for help nor the provision of information enabling officers immediately to end a threatening situation," we held that they were testimonial. ...

The basic purpose of the Confrontation Clause was to target the sort of abuses exemplified at the notorious treason trial of Sir Walter Raleigh. Thus, the most important instances in which the Clause restricts the introduction of out-of-court statements are those in which state actors are involved in a formal, out-of-court interrogation of a witness to obtain evidence for trial. Even where such an interrogation is conducted with all good faith, introduction of the resulting statements at trial can be unfair to the accused if they are untested by cross-examination. Whether formal or informal, out-of-court statements can evade the basic objective of the Confrontation Clause, which is to prevent the accused from being deprived of the opportunity to cross-examine the declarant about statements taken for use at trial. When, as in *Davis,* the primary purpose of an interrogation is to respond to an "ongoing emergency," its purpose is not to create a record for trial and thus is not within the scope of the Clause. But there may be *other* circumstances, aside from ongoing emergencies, when a statement is not procured with a primary purpose of creating an out-of-court substitute for trial testimony. In making the primary purpose determination, standard rules of hearsay, designed to identify some statements as reliable, will be relevant. Where no such primary purpose exists, the admissibility of a statement is the concern of state and federal rules of evidence, not the Confrontation Clause....

III

To determine whether the primary purpose of an interrogation is "to enable police assistance to meet an ongoing emergency," which would render the resulting statements nontestimonial, we objectively evaluate the circumstances in which the encounter occurs and the statements and actions of the parties.

A ...

An objective analysis of the circumstances of an encounter and the statements and actions of the parties to it provides the most accurate assessment of the "primary purpose of the interrogation." The circumstances in which an encounter occurs—*e.g.,* at or near the scene of the crime versus at a police station, during an ongoing emergency or afterwards—are clearly matters of objective fact. The statements and actions of the parties must also be objectively evaluated. That is, the relevant inquiry is not the subjective or actual purpose of the individuals involved in a particular encounter, but rather the purpose that reasonable participants would have had, as ascertained from the individuals' statements and actions and the circumstances in which the encounter occurred.

B

... The existence of an ongoing emergency is relevant to determining the primary purpose of the interrogation because an emergency focuses the participants on something other than proving past events potentially relevant to later criminal prosecution. Rather, it focuses them on ending a threatening situation. Implicit in *Davis* is the idea that because the prospect of fabrication in statements given for the primary purpose of resolving that emergency is presumably significantly diminished, the Confrontation Clause does not require such statements to be subject to the crucible of cross-examination.

This logic is not unlike that justifying the excited utterance exception in hearsay law. Statements "relating to a startling event or condition made while the declarant was under the stress of excitement caused by the event or condition," Fed. Rule Evid. 803(2); see also Mich. Rule Evid. 803(2) (2010), are considered reliable because the declarant, in the excitement, presumably cannot form a falsehood. An ongoing emergency has a similar effect of focusing an individual's attention on responding to the emergency.

[The question of whether an emergency exists] is a highly context-dependent inquiry.... Domestic violence cases like *Davis* and *Hammon* often have a narrower zone of potential victims than cases involving threats to public safety. An assessment of whether an emergency that threatens the police and public is ongoing cannot narrowly focus on whether the threat solely to the first victim has been neutralized because the threat to the first responders and public may continue.

The ... duration and scope of an emergency may depend in part on the type of weapon employed. The court relied on *Davis* and *Hammon,* in which the assailants used their fists, as controlling the scope of the emergency here, which involved the use of a gun. The problem with that reasoning is clear when considered in light of the assault on Amy Hammon. Hershel Hammon was armed only with his fists when he attacked his wife, so removing Amy to a separate room was sufficient to end the emergency. If Hershel had been reported to be armed with a gun, however, separation by a single household wall might not have been sufficient to end the emergency....

The medical condition of the victim is important to the primary purpose inquiry to the extent that it sheds light on the ability of the victim to have any purpose at all in responding to police questions and on the likelihood that any purpose formed would necessarily be a testimonial one. The victim's medical state also provides important context for first responders to judge the existence and magnitude of a continuing threat to the victim, themselves, and the public.

[None] of this suggests that an emergency is ongoing in every place or even just surrounding the victim for the entire time that the perpetrator of a violent crime is on the loose. [A] conversation which begins as an interrogation to determine the need for emergency assistance can evolve into testimonial statements. This evolution may occur if, for example, a declarant provides police with information that makes clear that what appeared to be an emergency is not or is no longer an emergency or that what appeared to be a public threat is actually a private dispute. It could also occur if a perpetrator is disarmed, surrenders, is apprehended, or, as in *Davis,* flees with little prospect of posing a threat to the public. Trial courts can determine in the first instance when any transition from nontestimonial to testimonial occurs, and exclude the portions of any statement that have become testimonial, as they do, for example, with unduly prejudicial portions of otherwise admissible evidence.

[Whether] an ongoing emergency exists is simply one factor—albeit an important factor—that informs the ultimate inquiry regarding the "primary purpose" of an interrogation. Another factor ... is the importance of *informality* in an encounter between a victim and police. [The] questioning in this case occurred in an exposed, public area, prior to the arrival of emergency medical services, and in a disorganized fashion. All of those facts make this case distinguishable from the formal station-house interrogation in *Crawford.*

C

In addition to the circumstances in which an encounter occurs, the statements and actions of both the declarant and interrogators provide objective evidence of the primary purpose of the interrogation.... In many instances, the primary purpose of the interrogation will be most accurately ascertained by looking to the contents of both the questions and the answers. To give an extreme example, if the police say to a victim, "Tell us who did this to you so that we can arrest and prosecute them," the victim's response that "Rick did it," appears purely accusatory because by virtue of the phrasing of the question, the victim necessarily has prosecution in mind when she answers.

The combined approach also ameliorates problems that could arise from looking solely to one participant. Predominant among these is the problem of mixed motives on the part of both interrogators and declarants. Police officers in our society function as both first responders and criminal investigators. Their dual responsibilities may mean that they act with different motives simultaneously or in quick succession. See New York v. Quarles, 467 U.S. 649 (1984) ("Undoubtedly most police officers [deciding whether to give *Miranda* warnings in a possible emergency situation] would act out of a host of different, instinctive, and largely unverifiable motives—their own safety, the safety of others, and perhaps as well the desire to obtain incriminating evidence from the suspect").

Victims are also likely to have mixed motives when they make statements to the police. During an ongoing emergency, a victim is most likely to want the threat to her and to other potential victims to end, but that does not necessarily mean that the victim wants or envisions prosecution of the assailant. A victim may want the attacker to be incapacitated temporarily or rehabilitated. Alternatively, a severely injured victim may have no purpose at all in answering questions posed; the answers may be simply reflexive. The victim's injuries could be so debilitating as to prevent her from thinking sufficiently clearly to understand whether her statements are for the purpose of addressing an ongoing emergency or for the purpose of future prosecution. ...

The dissent suggests that we intend to give controlling weight to the "intentions of the police." That is a misreading of our opinion. At trial, the declarant's statements, not the interrogator's questions, will be introduced to "establish the truth of the matter asserted," and must therefore pass the Sixth Amendment test. In determining whether a declarant's statements are testimonial, courts should look to all of the relevant circumstances.... The dissent criticizes the complexity of our approach, but we, at least, are unwilling to sacrifice accuracy for simplicity. Simpler is not always better, and courts making a "primary purpose" assessment should not be unjustifiably restrained from consulting all relevant information, including the statements and actions of interrogators. ...

IV

... As the context of this case brings into sharp relief, the existence and duration of an emergency depend on the type and scope of danger posed to the victim, the police, and the public. [The] scope of an emergency in terms of its threat to individuals other than the initial assailant and victim will often depend on the type of dispute involved. Nothing Covington said to the police indicated that the cause of the shooting was a purely private dispute or that the threat from the shooter had ended. The record reveals little about the motive for the shooting. The police officers who spoke with Covington at the gas station testified that Covington did not tell them what words Covington and Rick had exchanged prior to the shooting. What Covington did tell the officers was that he fled Bryant's back porch, indicating that he perceived an ongoing threat. The police did not know, and Covington did not tell them, whether the threat was limited to him. The potential scope of the dispute and therefore the emergency in this case thus stretches more broadly than those at issue in *Davis* and *Hammon* and encompasses a threat potentially to the police and the public.

This is also the first of our post-*Crawford* Confrontation Clause cases to involve a gun. The physical separation that was sufficient to end the emergency in *Hammon* was not necessarily sufficient to end the threat in this case; Covington was shot through the back door of Bryant's house. Bryant's argument that there was no ongoing emergency because "no shots were being fired" surely construes ongoing emergency too narrowly. An emergency does not last only for the time between when the assailant pulls the trigger and the bullet hits the victim. If an out-of-sight sniper pauses between shots, no one would say that the emergency ceases during the pause. That is an extreme example and not the situation here, but it serves to highlight the implausibility, at least as to certain weapons, of construing the emergency to last only precisely as long as the violent act itself, as some have construed our opinion in *Davis*.

At no point during the questioning did either Covington or the police know the location of the shooter. In fact, Bryant was not at home by the time the police searched his house at approximately 5:30 A.M. At some point between 3 A.M. and 5:30 A.M., Bryant left his house. At bottom, there was an ongoing emergency here where an armed shooter, whose motive for and location after the shooting were unknown, had mortally wounded Covington within a few blocks and a few minutes of the location where the police found Covington.

This is not to suggest that the emergency continued until Bryant was arrested in California a year after the shooting. We need not decide precisely when the emergency ended because Covington's encounter with the police and all of the statements he made during that interaction occurred within the first few minutes of the police officers' arrival and well before they secured the scene of the shooting—the shooter's last known location.

We reiterate, moreover, that the existence *vel non* of an ongoing emergency is not the touchstone of the testimonial inquiry; rather, the ultimate inquiry is whether the primary purpose of the interrogation was to enable police assistance to meet the ongoing emergency. We turn now to that inquiry, as informed by the circumstances of the ongoing emergency just described. The circumstances of the encounter provide important context for understanding Covington's statements to the police. When the police arrived at Covington's side, their first question to him was "What happened?" Covington's response was either "Rick shot me" or "I was shot," followed very quickly by an identification of "Rick" as the shooter. In response to further questions, Covington explained that the shooting occurred through the back door of Bryant's house and provided a physical description of the shooter. When he made the statements, Covington was lying in a gas station parking lot bleeding from a mortal gunshot wound to his abdomen. His answers to the police officers' questions were punctuated with questions about when emergency medical services would arrive. He was obviously in considerable pain and had difficulty breathing and talking. From this description of his condition and report of his statements, we cannot say that a person in Covington's situation would have had a "primary purpose" to establish or prove past events potentially relevant to later criminal prosecution.

For their part, the police responded to a call that a man had been shot. As discussed above, they did not know why, where, or when the shooting had occurred. Nor did they know the location of the shooter or anything else about the circumstances in which the crime occurred. The questions they asked—what had happened, who had shot him, and where the shooting occurred—were the exact type of questions necessary to allow the police to assess the situation, the threat to their own safety, and possible danger to the potential victim and to the public, including to allow them to ascertain whether they would be encountering a violent felon. In other words, they solicited the information necessary to enable them to meet an ongoing emergency....

Finally, we consider the informality of the situation and the interrogation. This situation is more similar, though not identical, to the informal, harried 911 call in *Davis* than to the structured, station-house interview in *Crawford*. As the officers' trial testimony reflects, the situation was fluid and somewhat confused: the officers arrived at different times; apparently each, upon arrival, asked Covington "what happened?"; and, contrary to the dissent's portrayal, they did not conduct a structured interrogation. The informality suggests that the interrogators' primary purpose was simply to address what they perceived to be an ongoing emergency, and the circumstances lacked any formality that would have alerted Covington to or focused him on the possible future prosecutorial use of his statements.

Because the circumstances of the encounter as well as the statements and actions of Covington and the police objectively indicate that the "primary purpose of the interrogation" was to enable police assistance to meet an ongoing emergency, Covington's identification and description of the shooter and the location of the shooting were not testimonial hearsay. The Confrontation Clause did not bar their admission at Bryant's trial.

For the foregoing reasons, we hold that Covington's statements were not testimonial and that their admission at Bryant's trial did not violate the Confrontation Clause. We leave for the Michigan courts to decide on remand whether the statements' admission was otherwise permitted by state hearsay rules....

THOMAS, J., concurring in the judgment.

I agree with the Court that the admission of Covington's out-of-court statements did not violate the Confrontation Clause, but I reach this conclusion because Covington's questioning by police lacked sufficient formality and solemnity for his statements to be considered "testimonial." ...

Rather than attempting to reconstruct the "primary purpose" of the participants, I would consider the extent to which the interrogation resembles those historical practices that the Confrontation Clause addressed. As the majority notes, Covington interacted with the police under highly informal circumstances, while he bled from a fatal gunshot wound. The police questioning was not "a formalized dialogue," did not result in "formalized testimonial materials" such as a deposition or affidavit, and bore no "indicia of solemnity." Nor is there any indication that the statements were offered at trial in order to evade confrontation. This interrogation bears little if any resemblance to the historical practices that the Confrontation Clause aimed to eliminate....

SCALIA, J., dissenting.

Today's tale—a story of five officers conducting successive

examinations of a dying man with the primary purpose, not of obtaining and preserving his testimony regarding his killer, but of protecting him, them, and others from a murderer somewhere on the loose—is so transparently false that professing to believe it demeans this institution. But reaching a patently incorrect conclusion on the facts is a relatively benign judicial mischief; it affects, after all, only the case at hand. In its vain attempt to make the incredible plausible, however—or perhaps as an intended second goal—today's opinion distorts our Confrontation Clause jurisprudence and leaves it in a shambles. Instead of clarifying the law, the Court makes itself the obfuscator of last resort. Because I continue to adhere to the Confrontation Clause that the People adopted, as described in Crawford v. Washington, 541 U.S. 36 (2004), I dissent.

I A ...

Crawford and *Davis* did not address whose perspective matters—the declarant's, the interrogator's, or both—when assessing "the primary purpose of [an] interrogation." In those cases the statements were testimonial from any perspective. I think the same is true here, but because the Court picks a perspective so will I: The declarant's intent is what counts. In-court testimony is more than a narrative of past events; it is a solemn declaration made in the course of a criminal trial. For an out-of-court statement to qualify as testimonial, the declarant must intend the statement to be a solemn declaration rather than an unconsidered or offhand remark; and he must make the statement with the understanding that it may be used to invoke the coercive machinery of the State against the accused. That is what distinguishes a narrative told to a friend over dinner from a statement to the police. The hidden purpose of an interrogator cannot substitute for the declarant's intentional solemnity or his understanding of how his words may be used.... (This does not mean the interrogator is irrelevant. The identity of an interrogator, and the content and tenor of his questions, can bear upon whether a declarant intends to make a solemn statement, and envisions its use at a criminal trial. But none of this means that the interrogator's purpose matters.)

In an unsuccessful attempt to make its finding of emergency plausible, the Court instead adopts a test that looks to the purposes of both the police and the declarant. ... The Court claims one affirmative virtue for its focus on the purposes of both the declarant and the police: It ameliorates problems that arise when declarants have "mixed motives." I am at a loss to know how. Sorting out the primary purpose of a declarant with mixed motives is sometimes difficult. But adding in the mixed motives of the police only compounds the problem. Now courts will have to sort through two sets of mixed motives to determine the primary purpose of an interrogation. And the Court's solution creates a mixed-motive problem where (under the proper theory) it does not exist—viz., where the police and the declarant each have one motive, but those motives conflict. ...

The only virtue of the Court's approach (if it can be misnamned a virtue) is that it leaves judges free to reach the "fairest" result under the totality of the circumstances. If the dastardly police trick a declarant into giving an incriminating statement against a sympathetic defendant, a court can focus on the police's intent and declare the statement testimonial. If the defendant "deserves" to go to jail, then a court can focus on whatever perspective is necessary to declare damning hearsay nontestimonial. And when all else fails, a court can mix-and-match perspectives to reach its desired outcome. Unfortunately, under this malleable approach the guarantee of confrontation is no guarantee at all.

B

Looking to the declarant's purpose (as we should), this is an absurdly easy case. ... From Covington's perspective, his statements had little value except to ensure the arrest and eventual prosecution of Richard Bryant. He knew the threatening situation had ended six blocks away and 25 minutes earlier when he fled from Bryant's back porch. Bryant had not confronted him face-to-face before he was mortally wounded, instead shooting him through a door. Even if Bryant had pursued him (unlikely), and after seeing that Covington had ended up at the gas station was unable to confront him there before the police arrived (doubly unlikely), it was entirely beyond imagination that Bryant would again open fire while Covington was surrounded by five armed police officers. And Covington knew the shooting was the work of a drug dealer, not a spree killer who might randomly threaten others....

Covington's pressing medical needs do not suggest that he was responding to an emergency, but to the contrary reinforce the testimonial character of his statements. He understood the police were focused on investigating a past crime, not his medical needs. [The officers] primarily asked questions with little, if any, relevance to Covington's dire situation. Police, paramedics, and doctors do not need to know the address where a shooting took place, the name of the shooter, or the shooter's height and weight to provide proper medical care. Underscoring that Covington understood the officers' investigative role, he interrupted their interrogation to ask "when is EMS coming?" When, in other words, would the focus shift to his medical needs rather than Bryant's crime? ...

C

Worse still for the repute of today's opinion, this is an absurdly easy case even if one (erroneously) takes the interrogating officers' purpose into account. The five officers interrogated Covington primarily to investigate past criminal events. None—absolutely none—of their actions indicated that they perceived an imminent threat. They did not draw their weapons, and indeed did not immediately search the gas station for potential shooters. To the contrary, all five testified that they questioned Covington *before conducting any investigation at the scene.* Would this have made any sense if they feared the presence of a shooter? Most tellingly, none of the officers started his interrogation by asking what would have been the obvious first question if any hint of such a fear existed: Where is the shooter? ...

At the very least, the officers' intentions *turned* investigative during their 10–minute encounter with Covington, and the conversation "evolved into testimonial statements." The fifth officer to arrive at the scene did not need to run straight to Covington and ask a battery of questions to determine the need for emergency assistance. He could have asked his fellow officers, who presumably had a better sense of that than Covington—and a better sense of what he could do to assist. No, the value of asking the same battery of questions a fifth time was to ensure that Covington told a consistent story and to see if any new details helpful to the investigation and eventual prosecution would emerge....

D ...

The Court's distorted view creates an expansive exception to the Confrontation Clause for violent crimes. Because Bryant posed a continuing threat to public safety in the Court's imagination, the emergency persisted for confrontation purposes at least until the police learned his motive for and location after the shooting. It may have persisted in this case until the police secured the scene of the shooting two-and-a-half hours later. (The relevance of securing the scene is unclear so long as the killer is still at large—especially if, as the Court speculates, he may be a spree-killer.) This is a dangerous definition of emergency. Many individuals who testify against a defendant at trial first offer their accounts to police in the hours after a violent act....

The 16th- and 17th-century English treason trials that helped inspire the Confrontation Clause show that today's decision is a mistake. The Court's expansive definition of an "ongoing emergency" and its willingness to consider the perspective of the interrogator and the declarant cast a more favorable light on those trials than history or our past decisions suggest they deserve. Royal officials conducted many of the *ex parte* examinations introduced against Sir Walter Raleigh and Sir John Fenwick while investigating alleged treasonous conspiracies of unknown scope, aimed at killing or overthrowing the King. Social stability in 16th- and 17th-century England depended mainly on the continuity of the ruling monarch, so such a conspiracy posed the most pressing emergency imaginable. Presumably, the royal officials investigating it would have understood the gravity of the situation and would have focused their interrogations primarily on ending the threat, not on generating testimony for trial. I therefore doubt that under the Court's test English officials acted improperly by denying Raleigh and Fenwick the opportunity to confront their accusers "face to face." ...

II

... But today's decision is not only a gross distortion of the facts. It is a gross distortion of the law—a revisionist narrative in which reliability continues to guide our Confrontation Clause jurisprudence, at least where emergencies and faux emergencies are concerned.

According to today's opinion, the *Davis* inquiry into whether a declarant spoke to end an ongoing emergency or rather to "prove past events potentially relevant to later criminal prosecution," is *not* aimed at answering whether the declarant acted as a witness. Instead, the *Davis* inquiry probes the *reliability* of a declarant's statements, implicitly importing the excited-utterances hearsay exception into the Constitution. A statement during an ongoing emergency is sufficiently reliable, the Court says, "because the prospect of fabrication ... is presumably significantly diminished," so it does not need to be subject to the crucible of cross-examination. Compare that with the holding of *Crawford:* "Where testimonial statements are at issue, the only indicium of reliability sufficient to satisfy constitutional demands is the one the Constitution actually prescribes: confrontation." 541 U.S., at 68–69. ...

The Court announces that in future cases it will look to "standard rules of hearsay, designed to identify some statements as reliable," when deciding whether a statement is testimonial. Ohio v. Roberts, 448 U.S. 56 (1980) said something remarkably similar: An out-of-court statement is admissible if it "falls within a firmly rooted hearsay exception" or otherwise bears adequate "indicia of reliability." We tried that approach to the Confrontation Clause for nearly 25 years before *Crawford rejected* it as an unworkable standard unmoored from the text and the historical roots of the Confrontation Clause. ...

The Court attempts to fit its resurrected interest in reliability into the *Crawford* framework, but the result is incoherent. Reliability, the Court tells us, is a good indicator of whether "a statement is ... an out-of-court substitute for trial testimony." That is patently false. Reliability tells us *nothing* about whether a statement is testimonial. Testimonial and nontestimonial statements alike come in varying degrees of reliability. An eyewitness's statements to the police after a fender-bender, for example, are both reliable and testimonial. Statements to the police from one driver attempting to blame the other would be similarly testimonial but rarely reliable.

The Court suggests otherwise because it misunderstands the relationship between qualification for one of the standard hearsay exceptions and exemption from the confrontation requirement. That relationship is not a causal one. Hearsay law exempts business records, for example, because businesses have a financial incentive to keep reliable records. See Fed. Rule Evid. 803(6). The Sixth Amendment also generally admits business records into evidence, but not because the records are reliable or because hearsay law says so. It admits them "because—having been created for the administration of an entity's affairs and not for the purpose of establishing or proving some fact at trial—they are not" weaker substitutes for live testimony. Melendez–Diaz v. Massachusetts, 129 S. Ct. 2527 (2009)....

The Court recedes from *Crawford* in a second significant way. It requires judges to conduct open-ended balancing tests and amorphous, if not entirely subjective, inquiries into the totality of the circumstances bearing upon reliability. Where the prosecution cries "emergency," the admissibility of a statement now turns on "a highly context-dependent inquiry" into the type of weapon the defendant wielded, the type of crime the defendant committed, the medical condition of the declarant, if the declarant is injured, whether paramedics have arrived on the scene,

166

whether the encounter takes place in an "exposed public area," whether the encounter appears disorganized, whether the declarant is capable of forming a purpose, whether the police have secured the scene of the crime, the formality of the statement, and finally, whether the statement strikes us as reliable. This is no better than the nine-factor balancing test we rejected in *Crawford*. I do not look forward to resolving conflicts in the future over whether knives and poison are more like guns or fists for Confrontation Clause purposes, or whether rape and armed robbery are more like murder or domestic violence. ...

In any case, we did not disavow multifactor balancing for reliability in *Crawford* out of a preference for rules over standards. We did so because it did violence to the Framers' design. It was judges' open-ended determination of what was reliable that violated the trial rights of Englishmen in the political trials of the 16th and 17th centuries. ... Not even the least dangerous branch can be trusted to assess the reliability of uncross-examined testimony in politically charged trials or trials implicating threats to national security.

Judicial decisions, like the Constitution itself, are nothing more than "parchment barriers," 5 Writings of James Madison 269, 272 (G. Hunt ed.1901). Both depend on a judicial culture that understands its constitutionally assigned role, has the courage to persist in that role when it means announcing unpopular decisions, and has the modesty to persist when it produces results that go against the judges' policy preferences....

Page 1323.   Insert this material at the end of note 3.

See also Bullcoming v. New Mexico, 131 S. Ct. 2705 (2011) (report describing a blood alcohol analysis was "testimonial" within the meaning of the Confrontation Clause because the report addressed chain of custody and certified the use of a precise testing protocol with the testing equipment; therefore the defendant in a DWI case had the right to confront at trial the analyst who certified the report).

Chapter 19

Sentencing

A. Who Sentences?

2. Legislative Sentencing

Page 1381.   Insert this material at the end of note 1.

See also Miller v. Alabama, 2012 WL 2368659 (June 25, 2012) (mandatory life imprisonment without parole for defendants under the age of 18 at the time of their crimes violates cruel and unusual punishment clause of Eighth Amendment).

C. Revisiting Pleas and Trials

1. Revisiting Proof at Trial

Page 1419.   Insert this material at the end of note 1.

See also Southern Union Company v. United States, 132 S. Ct. 2344 (applying Apprendi to imposition of criminal fine; judge erred in setting maximum potential fine of $38.1 million and imposing actual fine of $6 million because the decision engaged in judicial factfinding and enlarged maximum punishment defendant faced).

D. New Information about the Offender and the Victim

1. Offender Information

Page 1433. Insert this material at the end of note 4.

In Pepper v. United States, 131 S. Ct. 1229 (2011), the Supreme Court ruled that the sentencing judge, when resentencing a defendant after his initial sentence had been set aside on appeal, can consider evidence of the defendant's efforts at rehabilitation since the time of his initial sentencing. The defendant in this case demonstrated that he enrolled at a local community college as a full-time student and obtained part-time employment soon after his release from prison. Pepper also testified that he had recently married and was now supporting his wife and her daughter. Although a federal statute expressly bars the sentencing judge at resentencing from imposing a non-guideline sentence based on any factor other than those relied upon in the original sentence, the Court invalidated that statute under the Sixth Amendment principles described in United States v. Booker, 543 U.S. 220 (2005).

Chapter 20

Appeals

D. Retroactivity

Page 1521.   Insert this material at the end of note 1.

The Supreme Court discussed the relationship between retroactivity and the availability of the exclusionary rule remedy in Davis v. United States, 131 S. Ct. 2419 (2011) (exclusion not available as remedy for defendant when police reasonably relied on established precedent before a change in search and seizure doctrine, even if the new doctrine applies retroactively under *Griffith*).